Cards for
LADS and DADS

Elizabeth Moad

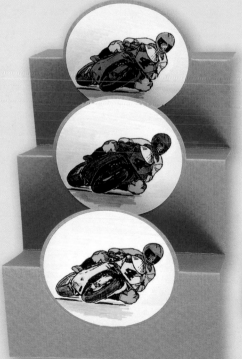

D&C
David and Charles

A DAVID & CHARLES BOOK
Copyright © David & Charles Limited 2006

David & Charles is an F+W Publications Inc. company
4700 East Galbraith Road
Cincinnati, OH 45236

First published in the UK in 2006

Text and project designs copyright © Elizabeth Moad 2006

Elizabeth Moad has asserted her right to be identified as author of this work in accordance
with the Copyright, Designs and Patents Act, 1988.

A catalogue record for this book is available from the British Library.

ISBN-13: 978-0-7153-2580-3 hardback
ISBN-10: 0-7153-2580-9 hardback

ISBN-13: 978-0-7153-2287-1 paperback
ISBN-10: 0-7153-2287-7 paperback

Printed in China by SNP Leefung
for David & Charles
Brunel House   Newton Abbot   Devon

Executive Editor Cheryl Brown
Editor Jennifer Proverbs
Art Editor Sarah Underhill
Designer Sarah Clark
Production Controller Ros Napper
Project Editor Jo Richardson
Photographer Karl Adamson

Visit our website at www.davidandcharles.co.uk

David & Charles books are available from all good bookshops; alternatively, you can
contact our Orderline on 0870 9908222 or write to us at FREEPOST EX2 110, D&C Direct,
Newton Abbot, TQ12 4ZZ (no stamp required UK only); US customers call 800-289-0963 and
Canadian customers call 800-840-5220.

*The author and publisher have made every effort to ensure that all the instructions
in the book are accurate and safe, and therefore cannot accept liability for any
resulting injury, damage or loss to persons or property, however it may arise.*

CONTENTS

IT'S A MAN THING!

Males make up around half the population, yet the overwhelming majority of ready-made greetings cards are targeted at women. Those that are male oriented are limited in both theme and design, which makes it hard to find a card appropriate for the particular man in your life. This book offers a whole variety of ideas for greetings cards to make for males of all ages, from lads to dads – and even great granddads!

It is a myth that men don't appreciate handmade cards – no one can fail to gain extra pleasure from a personalized design in which time and effort have been invested. Rather than struggling to fit the person to a standard, commercial design, here you are given the means to make a card that is unique to the recipient's interests, achievements or life event, with intriguing twists guaranteed to grab your man's attention.

SPORTING LIFE

Designs representing a wide variety of popular sporting activities are featured in this section, including ball and racket games and team sports, which will appeal to sport spectators and players alike, as well as more solitary pursuits.

INDOOR LEISURE

There is something to suit every male here, whether their recreational interests lie in the cultural or creative, the practical or the skilful or in the mind-challenging or imagination-stimulating!

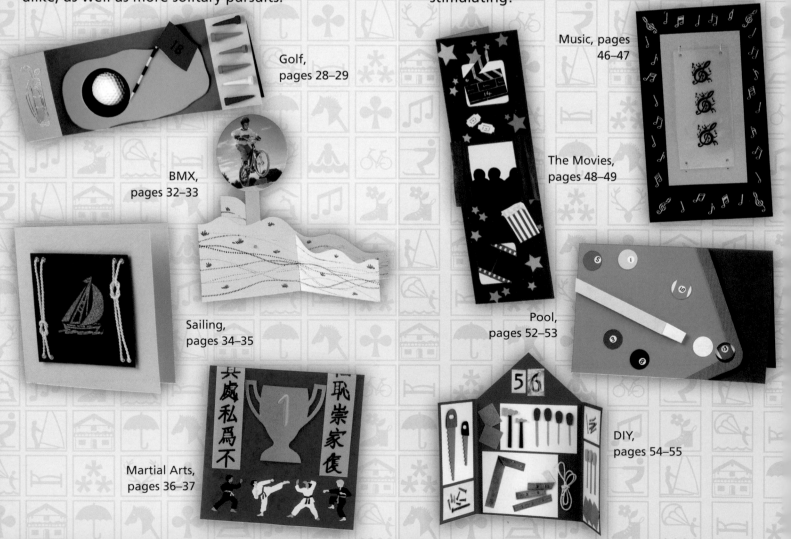

Golf,
pages 28–29

BMX,
pages 32–33

Sailing,
pages 34–35

Martial Arts,
pages 36–37

Music, pages
46–47

The Movies,
pages 48–49

Pool,
pages 52–53

DIY,
pages 54–55

With the widespread popularity of scrapbooking and other papercrafts, there are hundreds of interesting printed papers, exciting peel-off stickers and inventive embellishments, as well as clever tools, for you to make truly creative cards for men. The following pages present a practical guide to choosing and using these materials and equipment, including demonstrations of basic and more advanced craft techniques. You can then select from a range of innovative card designs, grouped thematically into four chapters (see below), which can all be tailor-made for that main man by incorporating personal details such as names, ages, messages and photographs. Each chapter also includes a gallery showcasing additional design ideas. A section at the back of the book contains all the templates you will need to make up the cards (see pages 96–109), plus a card-giver's index (see page 112) for speedy selection of a special occasion or theme.

OUTDOOR LEISURE

Those males that have a taste for speed, action and adventure are well catered for in this section, but others who like the more leisurely pace of the past or of nature will also be satisfied.

SPECIAL CELEBRATIONS

This section includes cards for marking a male's major milestones of life, as well as specially male-oriented designs to celebrate the key events of the calendar year in appropriate style.

Gardening, pages 62–63

Formula 1, pages 66–67

Skiing, pages 64–65

Holidays, pages 72–73

Father's Day, pages 78–79

New Home, pages 86–87

Christmas, pages 88–89

Retirement, pages 92–93

WITH MEN IN MIND

There is a bewilderingly huge array of materials for handcrafting cards on offer, but if you approach the selection process with men in mind, you will soon narrow down the choice and be well on the way to giving a masculine edge to your card designs. And you don't have to spend masses of money to make fantastic cards for men. Keep on the lookout for suitable everyday items and you will soon find that you have built up a treasure trove of materials for the men in your life, to dip into whenever you need.

PAPERS

Machine-printed papers and card are available in most art and craft shops in plain single colours, which provide an essential foundation for all card making, but if you shop around scrapbooking suppliers, craft shops and hobby shows, you will soon find a wealth of printed papers that are ideal for men.

- Materials for scrapbooking offer themed booklets of printed papers, from which you can cut out specific male-oriented images, as well as good-value pads of patterned papers.

- Printed papers specially designed for use in découpage are another handy source of images, including those relating to particular male-dominated sports or hobbies, or more general suitable subjects such as gardening.

- Giftwrapping paper is a widely available source of images and patterns appropriate for men's cards.

STENCILS

The book provides you with many templates for making the featured designs (see pages 96–109), from which you can make your own stencils to use again and again in all kinds of designs (see Castles, page 76).

- You can buy booklets of stencils, containing several different designs or motifs on a particular theme, which can be used repeatedly.

- Plastic stencils specially designed for embossing with intricate details can also be used by carefully sponging colour through them (see page 13).

BRIGHT SPARK
PUNCHES ARE IDEAL FOR CREATING STENCILS — THE PUNCHED-OUT SHAPE CAN BE SPONGED AROUND WITH COLOUR OR THE 'NEGATIVE' SHAPE LEFT AFTER PUNCHING COULD BE SPONGED THROUGH.

PEEL-OFF STICKERS

These come in a variety of sophisticated designs, continually being added to, and are ideal for creating instant cards for men. They are also available in a range of different forms, such as outline, solid and embossed, as well as different styles of numbers and borders.

■ Scrapbooking suppliers offer an excellent range of themed sets of peel-off stickers, including a significant proportion of suitably male subjects.

■ Venture into children's stationery departments or even toy shops, where you can often find a fund of fun peel-off stickers.

■ Make your own stickers using a Xyron™ machine with an adhesive cartridge (see page 14) to apply glue to the reverse of punched or cutout shapes.

EMBELLISHMENTS

An embellishment is anything that is used to decorate a card, but usually refers to non-paper items, such as metal charms, hinges, skeleton leaves, photo mounts, cords, etc., available from craft shops or suppliers. They may seem quite expensive, but a packet of metal charms, for example, can be divided among several cards.

■ Look for card-making potential in everyday items at the supermarket, or those that might trigger a design idea – such as a packet of wooden kebab sticks, used for a flagpole in Fourth of July, page 95, and to coil card for a corkscrew in Wine, page 44.

■ Sewing materials are another good source of embellishments, and they don't have to be new, but preferably from or for men's clothing – buttons, shoelaces, threads and scraps of fabric, for instance.

BRIGHT SPARK
LOOK IN THRIFT OR CHARITY SHOPS FOR PACKETS OF USED STAMPS OR OLD ROAD MAPS AND PICTURE BOOKS TO CUT UP AND USE IN YOUR CARD DESIGNS.

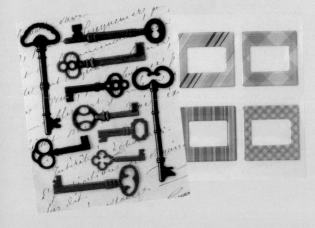

WORKBENCH ESSENTIALS

Buy the minimum amount of tools and equipment that you need – stick to the essentials. It is best to invest in a few good-quality items from which you can extract the maximum use – you may, for instance, be able to use one tool for a number of different craft techniques. When visiting craft shops and shows, select carefully and don't get so carried away that you blow your budget on items that sit collecting dust on a shelf.

BRIGHT SPARK
BUILD UP YOUR ARMOURY OF MORE SPECIALIST TOOLS AND EQUIPMENT GRADUALLY AND THOUGHTFULLY OVER TIME BY ASKING FOR SPECIFIC ITEMS AS GIFTS.

BASIC TOOL KIT

Before you begin any card making, it is a good idea to assemble a basic tool kit and keep it organized, well-stocked and to hand.

scissors ■ craft knife ■ metal ruler ■ sharp HB pencil ■ white pencil ■ pencil eraser ■ empty ballpoint pen or scoring tool ■ bone folder ■ cutting mat ■ foam pad ■ paintbrushes ■ wooden clothes peg ■ PVA (white) glue, dish and cocktail sticks ■ glue stick ■ adhesive tape ■ double-sided adhesive tape ■ low-tack adhesive tape ■ adhesive foam pads ■ spray glue and old cardboard box ■ superglue ■ scrap paper and card

CUTTING TOOLS

Making a choice of cutting tools is mostly a case of finding what you like to use and feel comfortable with.

◀ SCISSORS

Essentially, you need a large pair for trimming and a small pair for intricate work. Keep the blades clean and sharp.

▼ FANCY-EDGED SCISSORS

These have blades with a decorative edge, ideal for cutting fancy borders and jazzing up edges.

▲ CUTTING MAT

A self-healing cutting mat is essential – when cut vertically with a craft knife, the edges of the cut come together again, or heal, so as not to leave an indent.

▼ CRAFT KNIVES

Use for cutting longer straight edges. Always use a craft knife with a metal ruler – the knife can cut nicks in a plastic one, making it unusable – and on a cutting mat to protect your work surface. Replace blades regularly to ensure a clean cut. If the craft knife does not have a retractable blade, always stick the blade into a cork to prevent accidents.

PAPER TRIMMERS OR GUILLOTINES

These come in a wide variety from large to small and from cheap to expensive. While not essential, they do save time and effort, and produce a clean, straight cut every time.

GLUES

Different types of glue and adhesive are required in card making for particular purposes, so it is important to keep a range in your kit to achieve the best results.

▶ PVA (WHITE) GLUE

This inexpensive water-based, all-purpose glue becomes transparent when dry, and is best used for delicate work, applied with the tip of a cocktail stick (see right).

▶ GLUE STICKS

These tubes of solid glue, which can be rubbed over large areas, are good for applying an even coat of adhesive that won't make the paper soggy.

GLITTER GLUES

These are available in a wide range of colours and are intended for decorative purposes only.

SUPERGLUE

This is useful when you need a long-lasting adhesion and for gluing heavier-weight embellishments to cards, such as wiggly eyes and polymer clay. It is very powerful and must be used with extreme care. Keep it well out of reach of children. It will also mark work surfaces.

▶ DOUBLE-SIDED ADHESIVE TAPE

Pieces or lengths of this tape are cut and stuck down, then the backing strip removed to reveal the second adhesive surface. It is ideal for mounting work behind an aperture.

◀ ADHESIVE FOAM PADS

Available in a block of small pads or individual larger pads, these are sticky on both sides and raise whatever is glued to them away from the surface to give a 3-D effect.

◀ CLEAR ADHESIVE DOTS

Available in different sizes and thicknesses, these easy-to-use dots come on a paper strip that is simply pressed face down onto the required area.

BRIGHT SPARK
Use repositional clear adhesive dots to temporarily adhere items, for instance when trying out an arrangement of elements on a card.

▶ SILICONE GEL

This clear gel, applied direct from the tube, both glues and adds depth. It dries clear and solid, making it suitable for 3-D découpage and other crafting purposes where adhesive foam pads may not be suitable.

▶ SPRAY GLUE

Useful for sticking larger pieces of card or paper, the permanent form gives excellent bonding and is used when a complete and even covering of glue is required.

HEALTH AND SAFETY

- Always use aerosol sprays in a well-ventilated room or even outside – additionally, spray glue is best used inside an old cardboard box.
- Always read the manufacturer's instructions when using products such as polymer clay or shrink plastic.

CREATIVE BASICS

A few simple items will bring shape and colour to even the simplest card designs.

▶ SPONGES AND SPONGE DAUBERS

These can be used to apply ink to a variety of surfaces and can achieve many different textures.

INKPADS

Create a basic colour palette with a range of inkpads – as well as being used for rubber stamping, they are a no-fuss alternative to paint for applying colour. See pages 16–17 for further details.

▶ WATERCOLOUR PENCILS AND FELT-TIP PENS

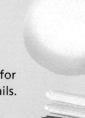

It is surprising how many times you will use these pencils and pens in your projects, so invest in a packet of each in a variety of colours.

▶ PUNCHES

These are a quick way of making identical shapes and come in all sorts of designs and sizes, including corner or border punches. Circle punches are particularly versatile – for instance, use to make tyres (see Formula 1, page 66), balls (see Pool, page 52) or a flower face (see Get Well, page 95).

DOING THE GROUNDWORK

Although you can buy pre-cut cards of many shapes and sizes, you may wish to make your own from a special piece of card or you may have a card that you want to use but it does not have an aperture. Uneven cutting can really stand out, and if you notice that something is not quite straight, then the recipient will too. Handmade cards should still look professional, so follow the instructions for this and other basic card-crafting techniques presented here to achieve the desired results.

SCORING AND FOLDING

Scoring paper allows it to be folded more easily, and results in a crisper fold.

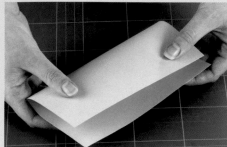

1 Use an HB pencil to make two pencil marks where you want the score line on the wrong side of the paper and line up the ruler with these marks. Draw an empty ball-point pen or scoring tool all the way along the line so that the paper is indented. The scored line will become the inside of the fold.

2 Use both hands to fold the paper or card along the score line.

3 Use a bone folder on its side to press along the fold line to make it sharp. The back of a clean metal spoon could be used in place of a bone folder.

CUTTING

The cleanest cuts are made with a flat, clean surface, a sharp craft knife and metal ruler and a steady hand. The ruler below has a non-slip surface on the underside, which helps to keep it in place on the paper.

1 Working on a cutting mat, use an HB pencil and a metal ruler to make two pencil marks on the paper where you want to cut if you are cutting a small piece, or make three pencil marks if large. Place your metal ruler along the cutting line and stand, putting downward pressure on the ruler to hold it firmly in place, while you draw the knife towards you in a single movement. Make sure that the section you want to use is under the ruler, so if the knife should slip, it will cut into the waste part.

2 Keep the blade of the craft knife at a 45-degree angle when cutting. Draw the knife across the paper, but don't press too hard or the paper will wrinkle and an uneven edge will be left. When cutting thick paper, draw the blade across once without too much pressure, then again with more pressure to make the final cut.

BRIGHT SPARK
If the sheet is large, mark the cutting line with three pencil marks and cut about 20cm (8in). Keeping the knife in the paper, move your other hand down the ruler, press firmly down and continue cutting – repeat several times using a long metal ruler if very large.

TEARING

As an alternative to cutting, a torn edge adds an interesting dimension and can break up an otherwise uniform edge. When tearing paper, you will need to take into account the grain of the paper. If you are not sure of the grain of a particular paper, test first by tearing a small piece of the paper.

TEARING WITH THE GRAIN

Tearing with the grain is easy and can produce a relatively straight line, as the paper naturally wants to tear this way.

TEARING AGAINST THE GRAIN

Tearing against the grain is harder and produces more uneven tears.

TEARING WITH A RULER

If straight but torn lines are required, use a ruler as a guide. Hold the ruler firmly with one hand and pull the paper up and towards you with the other hand.

EYELETS

These are used to attach panels to cards, thread cord through or as a purely decorative embellishment. You will need a special eyelet holepunch to make a hole of the right size for the eyelet, an eyelet setting tool and a hammer (see page 14).

1 Using an HB pencil, mark on the card where you wish the eyelets to be placed. Place the card on an old cutting mat and place the eyelet holepunch over the pencil mark. Hammer down onto the tool to punch a hole.

2 Insert the eyelet into the punched hole. The side on which you are about to hammer is the wrong side of the eyelet, so make sure that the eyelet is on the side you want it to be.

3 Place the setting tool over the eyelet. Hit the top of the setting tool with the hammer to flatten the back of the eyelet.

4 The backs of the eyelets should be rounded and as smooth against the card as possible. Once eyelets are set, they cannot be removed.

SAFE AND SECURE
These eyelets provide the perfect finish to this drawbridge, allowing it to be raised and lowered without damaging the card itself (see page 86).

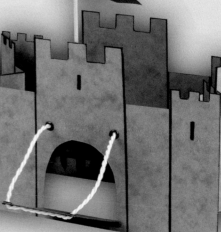

CUTTING AND MOUNTING APERTURES

An aperture is the hole cut out of a piece of paper or card. A single-fold or a two-fold card may have an aperture – either in a pre-cut card (see Wine, page 44) or one you have cut yourself (see The Movies, page 48). The advantage of using a single-fold card with an aperture is that it lets the light through whatever is placed in the aperture. A two-fold card has three panels, with the aperture in the central panel. The third panel is folded over to cover the reverse of the insert.

CUTTING

1 Using an HB pencil and ruler, draw the aperture you wish to cut out onto paper or card. Use a set square to ensure that the corners are right angles.

2 Using a sharp craft knife and metal ruler on a cutting mat, carefully cut along your first marked line. The ruler should be on the good area of the paper or card so that if the knife slips it cuts into the central portion, which will be removed. Turn the paper round for each cut so that you draw the knife towards you on each cut. Make sure that your cuts don't extend beyond your marked lines.

BRIGHT SPARK

WHEN YOU HAVE CUT ALL FOUR SIDES OF THE APERTURE, IF THE CENTRAL PORTION FAILS TO FALL AWAY, USE THE CRAFT KNIFE TO CUT THE CORNERS CAREFULLY SO THAT IT DOES SO. DO NOT PULL IT OUT OR YOU WILL TEAR OR DAMAGE THE CORNERS.

MOUNTING

1 Ensure that the paper panel insert is at least 1cm (³/₈in) larger than the aperture. Place lengths of double-sided adhesive tape around the aperture window on the inside of the card – a two-fold card has been used here. Remove the backing from the tape and place the insert, right side down, onto the tape, then press down firmly. You may find it easier to position the paper by turning the card over so that you can see the right side and holding it over the work you want to insert.

2 Turn the card right side down and place lengths of double-sided adhesive tape along the four edges of the central panel. Remove the backing and fold the third panel over the wrong side of the insert. Press firmly so that all parts are well stuck down. You now have a single-fold card. Glue – either a glue stick or PVA (white) glue – can be used instead and will allow you to move the insert slightly if it has been positioned incorrectly.

USING ADHESIVE FOAM PADS

Adhesive foam pads can also be used for mounting, which will lift the image from its background.

BRIGHT SPARK

BY USING MORE THAN ONE LAYER OF ADHESIVE FOAM PADS FOR MOUNTING, YOU CAN CREATE EXTRA DEPTH. SEE POOL, PAGE 52, WHERE THEY HAVE BEEN USED ONCE TO ATTACH THE POOL TABLE, THEN AGAIN TO ATTACH THE CUE.

SPONGING

You can apply ink from a piece of sponge, sponge dauber or direct from an inkpad through stencils, around shapes or along the edges of a card for interesting effects (see below). By lightly applying ink, sponging can be used to create soft backgrounds, or a stronger feature can be made using more ink.

USING STENCILS

Cut or punch an aperture in the shape of your choice from scrap card and place over a piece of coloured paper. Press a piece of sponge into an inkpad, then dab through the aperture onto the paper, to create a square or other shape of colour. The aperture can be repositioned on the paper and inked in the same way to make further shapes, to create a pattern.

OUTLINING SHAPES

Cut out a card template of a motif, in this case a running shoe. Place the template on a piece of coloured paper. Using a sponge dauber – a mini sponge in a holder that fits onto the end of your finger – dab into an inkpad, then dab ink around the template. The sponge dauber allows greater control over where the ink is placed – here, only around the edge of the template, to create an outline effect.

CREATING BORDERS

Tear a piece of scrap paper and place parallel to one edge of a sheet of coloured paper, in this case blue, leaving a border of blue paper. Dab the sponge of a light blue inkpad over the torn edge of the scrap paper onto the blue paper. Continue sponging all the way along the torn edge. Move the blue paper around to sponge the other edges in the same way, to create a soft border. Discard the scrap paper.

TEMPLATES

You will find templates for all the shapes and stencils used in the card designs on pages 96–109. These are mostly printed actual size, so are ready to use, but the templates on pages 108–109 need to be enlarged on a photocopier set at 200% enlargement.

1 Using an HB pencil and tracing paper, trace the chosen image from the template or photocopy the image onto paper. Cut around the image using scissors.

2 Place the paper template on scrap card – cardboard from an empty cereal packet is just the right thickness. Using a pencil and holding the paper in place, draw around the paper template.

3 Cut out the image from the cardboard to form the template. Discard the paper template, as this is not sturdy enough. Label and store your cardboard templates in plastic sleeves in a ringbinder for future use.

GET IN SHAPE
Careful preparation of templates allows you to produce cards that go further every time (see page 70).

POWER TOOLS

If you enjoy card making and decide to make it a hobby, or even a paying hobby, there are several tools that save time and help to achieve a professional result.

▼ SHAPE TEMPLATES AND CUTTING TOOL

Plastic templates of various shapes and sizes are used in conjunction with a cutter to cut apertures and shapes or crop photographs (see BMX, page 32) – difficult shapes, such as circles, can be more easily cut than with a craft knife.

▼ EMBOSSING SYSTEMS

There are various embossing systems available, such as the Fiskars® ShapeBoss™, that avoid the use of a lightbox and so are very easy to use – see page 19.

▼ EYELETS AND EYELET SETTING TOOLS

Eyelets are a versatile embellishment, and come in a variety of sizes and colours, as well as shapes, although the most common are round. The setting tools comprise a holepunch, setting tool and hammer (see page 11).

▶ XYRON™ MACHINE

A multi-purpose gadget: by inserting an adhesive cartridge, it can apply an even coating of glue to paper shapes, while a magnetic/laminate cartridge applies a magnetic backing and a clear plastic layer to the top of paper (see Formula 1, page 66), and a double-sided laminate cartridge applies a clear plastic layer to both the bottom and top (see Retirement, page 92).

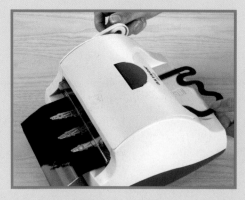

BRIGHT SPARK
If you have crafting friends, why not share more specialist/expensive tools or borrow a tool from a friend and 'try before you buy'.

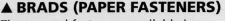

▲ BRADS (PAPER FASTENERS)

These metal fasteners, available in a wide variety of shapes, sizes and colours, are useful for attaching materials to cards that are difficult to glue, but they can also be purely decorative (see Gardening, page 62). A hole is punched in the paper or card, the prongs pushed through the hole and then bent outwards to flatten on the back of the paper or card.

▲ POLYMER CLAY

This moulding material comes in blocks of colour that can be blended together to make other shades. Once moulded, the clay is baked in an oven according to the manufacturer's instructions, when it becomes completely solid (see Golf, page 28).

▲ 3-D PAINT

This very thick liquid paint, applied directly from the tube, comes in many colours and can be used on most surfaces, even fabric, to give dimension and texture (see The Movies, page 48). It should be left overnight to dry, but always remember to check the manufacturer's instructions.

▲ PUFF PAINT

This is left to dry for a few hours or overnight, then heated with a hairdryer or heat gun. As the paint heats, it puffs up and changes texture (see Steam Trains, page 74).

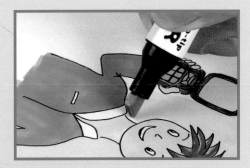

▲ MARKER PENS

These dual-tipped permanent marker pens, used by professional graphic artists, are much easier to use than regular felt-tip pens and achieve a better result (see Manga, page 56).

▼ RIBBLER

Paper strips are fed between the ribbler's patterned cogs (in this case wavy), and by turning the handle, the cogs rotate and the paper is drawn through and pressed into shape (see Holidays, page 72).

▲ CLEAR RESIN WINDOWS

Also called page pebbles or dome stickers, these are sticky-backed, raised embellishments that can be placed over peel-off stickers or images to highlight them (see Artist, page 42).

BUILDING SITE

The following more specialist techniques offer you the opportunity to build on your basic skills to add further creative interest to your cards. Each technique has many applications, and can be used in combination, giving you almost limitless design potential.

RUBBER STAMPING

Rubber stamping is a fast way of printing identical images onto paper. The designs come pre-cut into rubber and mounted onto a wooden block or foam pad for easy handling. The stamp is inked using an inkpad or brush marker, then pressed onto paper to transfer the image. Once dry, the image can be coloured using pencils, felt-tip pens or inks.

1 Inkpads are often smaller than the stamp, but this is not a problem. Rather than applying the stamp to the inkpad, do the reverse. Hold the stamp in one hand, design uppermost. Take a single-colour inkpad in the other hand and dab it over the design. Dab the inkpad over the design several times to apply an even coating of ink.

2 An even coating of ink is left on the stamp and no ink has touched the edge of the rubber or wooden block. If ink does get on the block, wipe off carefully with kitchen paper before printing, particularly if there is ink on the surrounding rubber, as this may transfer to the paper when printed.

3 Hold the stamp over the paper where you want the image, press the stamp evenly onto the paper and lift the stamp off immediately. It is important to work on a perfectly flat surface.

4 Try to clean your stamps immediately after use by placing two pieces of damp kitchen paper on a saucer and pressing the stamp onto the paper several times. Dry the stamp with clean, dry kitchen paper. Some inks, such as solvent inks, cannot be cleaned with water and require a special stamp cleaner – buy this when you purchase the inkpad.

STAMP YOUR MARK
From simple cricket bats to an intricate grapevine border, stamps allow you to create all kinds of images (see pages 26 and 44).

RUBBER-STAMP HEAT EMBOSSING

Embossing in the context of rubber stamping means something different to other forms of embossing. Here, it refers to the technique of heating embossing powder, which then melts to become raised and shiny. Rubber stamps can be used with clear or tinted embossing inkpads. Alternatively, a dual-tipped embossing pen can be used to draw freehand designs or straight lines.

1 Stamp or draw your design onto paper (see above).

2 Sprinkle embossing powder all over the design. Apply the embossing powder liberally so that the whole design is covered and no parts are missed.

3 Stand the paper with the design upright and shake off the excess embossing powder onto scrap paper. The wetness of the ink will hold the powder in place on the design.

4 Tip the excess embossing powder back into the container by making a funnel shape with the scrap paper.

5 Place the paper with the design on a ceramic tile or heatproof surface and heat using a heat gun. Hold the heat gun about 10cm (4in) away from the image. Watch the embossing powder melt to a semi-liquid form, then remove the heat gun and switch off. The paper can be held in place with a wooden clothes peg, to keep your fingers well away from the heat gun.

▲ **CHARACTERFUL**
Heat embossing gives this simple oriental design texture and shine for an eye-catching finish (see page 37).

INKPAD AND STAMP MAINTENANCE

- When you have finished using a stamp, make sure that it is clean and thoroughly dry before storing away from direct sunlight.

- If there are any parts of the stamp that you cannot clean with kitchen paper, use an old toothbrush to remove any ink residue.

- With all types of inkpads and pens, replace the lids or caps immediately after use, otherwise they will dry out.

- Dye-based inkpads with a felt inkpad should be stored upside down, allowing the ink to travel to the surface of the pad.

► **TIME TO SHINE**
A dual-tipped embossing pen and a metal ruler were used to create the straight lines of the 'inlay' (see page 58).

QUILLING

Sometimes called paper filigree, quilling is the craft of coiling thin strips of paper, which are then glued and pinched into different shapes. A quilling tool is used to make the coils.

CLOSED COILS

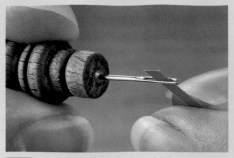  

1 Holding the quilling tool in one hand, with the other hand, slot one end of a 20cm (8in) length of 3mm (1/8in) wide paper through the metal prongs. Only feed 5mm (3/16in) through the prongs to start with, as this is just enough to hold the paper when turning the tool.

2 Rotate the quilling tool, keeping the paper taut with the other hand. As you turn the quilling tool, the paper is wound around the tool, forming a tight circle of paper, but the tension must be constantly maintained with the other hand.

3 Remove the quilling tool from the centre of the tight coil. Using a cocktail stick, apply a dab of PVA (white) glue to the end of the paper strip. Press this glued end to the coil to prevent it unwinding. This is a tight closed coil because the paper strip has not been allowed to unwind at all before the end was glued in place.

LOOSE CLOSED COILS

Experiment by allowing the coil to unwind a little before gluing the end in place, to make a loose closed coil.

BASIC CLOSED COIL SHAPES

This is a selection of coils made from 20cm (8in) lengths of 3mm (1/8in) wide paper. At the top right is a tight coil, while the other coils were made by letting the coil unwind by different amounts before gluing, to create different sizes.

PINCHING

Pinch one end of a loose closed coil with your fingers, to form a teardrop shape. It could be pinched again to form a multitude of shapes, such as the examples shown here.

GET A RAISE
The 3-D effect achieved with quilling adds an unexpected twist to many designs.

EMBOSSING

Embossing is a complicated term in crafting because it can mean several different techniques. Here, embossing refers to the technique of making a raised image on paper by applying pressure. The fibres of the paper are stretched to make a new shape, but the colour does not change as it does in parchment craft. The following embossing technique does not necessitate the use of a metal stencil over a lightbox.

1 With this Fiskars® ShapeBoss™ stencil set, there are two identical plastic stencils, labelled top and bottom. These are secured in the tray with pegs. Lift up the stencil labelled 'top' and insert a sheet of paper in between the two stencil layers.

2 Position the paper under the design to be embossed. Using the large ball embossing tool, apply a consistent downward pressure and outline the stencil design. There is no need to emboss the centre of the design.

3 Move the paper around between the stencil layers to emboss all over the paper, a border or wherever you wish.

4 Remove the paper from the stencil and turn over. Where you have embossed will be raised and this is the right side of the paper. Remember when embossing letters or numbers that the design will appear back to front while working.

BRIGHT SPARK
IF THE EMBOSSING TOOL DOES NOT GLIDE OVER THE PAPER EASILY, YOU CAN RUB IT ON WAXED PAPER OR YOUR HAND TO LUBRICATE IT SLIGHTLY.

WHAT A RELIEF!
By embossing shapes randomly over a card, you can create an interesting textured background (see page 80).

PARCHMENT CRAFT

This craft uses specialist translucent papers that change colour when pressure is applied. The essence of parchment craft is varying the amount of pressure applied through embossing to control the shade and tone produced.

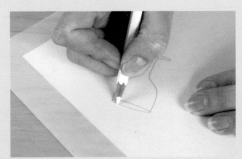

1 Place the sheet of parchment paper over the chosen design. Using a white pencil, trace over the design.

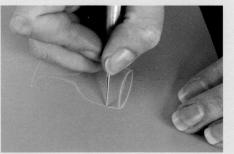

2 Place the parchment paper with the traced design on a foam pad and emboss the outline using a fine or medium ball embossing tool. If you are embossing numbers or letters, turn the parchment paper over before embossing so that you are working on the reverse side.

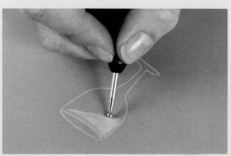

3 With the large ball embossing tool, emboss the design by rubbing the tool over the area you wish to become whiter, using a side-to-side motion. Turn the paper over periodically to see how white the right side is looking.

YOU'VE GOT MALE...

As well as providing extra protection during transit in the mail or any other method of delivery, bespoke presentation and packaging can be used to complement and enhance your handmade cards for men, giving them extra male appeal. Envelopes and boxes, tailored to fit any size of item, can be customized or coordinated with the card inside, and incorporate additional features, such as a matching gift tag or label.

ENVELOPE

The great advantage of making your own envelopes is that you don't need to limit your card design to a standard size to fit a ready-made envelope, so you can let your imagination run wild and make an envelope to fit the card when you have finished it. Use paper that is strong yet will fold neatly.

1 Enlarge the template on page 109 on a photocopier at 200%, or to whatever size you require. Cut out along the outside solid lines, then draw around the template onto scrap card and cut out using scissors. Keep and use the template as many times as you need. Draw around the template onto your chosen paper and cut out with scissors.

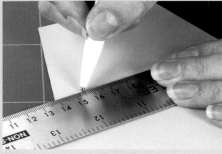

2 Place the envelope, right side down, on a cutting mat. Using an empty ballpoint pen or scoring tool against a metal ruler, score along the dashed lines across the flaps marked on the template on page 109.

3 Use a glue stick to run a line of glue along the two side edges of one of the larger flaps. Fold the two smaller side flaps inwards and press the glued flap onto these.

ENVELOPE TEMPLATES AND LINERS

If you envisage making envelopes frequently or a large amount, you can purchase clear plastic envelope templates that are more hard-wearing than card, and some of these offer three different sizes on a single template to choose from to match your card. Use a printed paper to coordinate with your card design.

1 Place the clear plastic envelope template on your chosen paper. If it is printed paper with a busy design, use the plain side. Draw around the template onto the paper. Here, a liner for the envelope was made by cutting out a larger envelope and then a smaller envelope from printed paper.

2 Place the liner inside the larger envelope and use a glue stick to glue in place. Fold the two outer flaps inwards. Fold the lower flap upwards. Apply glue to the two folded flaps, then press the lower flap down onto the two folded flaps.

BRIGHT SPARK

Instead of making a separate liner, use a plain paper for the envelope, then print on the inside with a rubber stamp, such as the lips stamp on page 84, to create a pattern before gluing the envelope sides in place.

POST-WISE

- A design covering the entire envelope should be worked in light colours, so as not to interfere with the address and postmark.
- Ensure that the address is clearly visible through the design.
- Charms and trinkets should be limited to the card inside.

CARD BOX

Card boxes are sturdier than envelopes and are more suitable where a card has raised embellishments that need protecting. Strong paper or card can be used for card boxes.

1 Enlarge the template on page 108 on a photocopier at 200%, or to whatever size you require. Cut out along the outside solid lines, then draw around the template onto scrap card and cut out using a craft knife and metal ruler. Draw around the card template onto your chosen paper or card and cut out in the same way.

2 Place the box, right side down, on a cutting mat. Using an empty ballpoint pen or scoring tool against a metal ruler, score along the dashed lines marked on the template on page 108.

3 Using a glue stick, apply glue to the right side of the four tabs on the box base. Press these tabs to the inside of the box sides to form the box base. The lid of the box will then fit neatly into the base.

◄ PUT A TIE ON
A box for a sailing card (see page 34) is tied with blue cord using a reef knot.

▼► DRESS TO IMPRESS
These boxes are colour coordinated with the cards inside (see pages 72 and 28). The outside can be decorated if hand delivered. If posting, place bubble wrap inside and use strong card. The box dimensions have been changed to fit the long, thin Golf card.

PERSONALIZE A MESSAGE

Many people tend to panic at the thought of writing on their card, but there are many creative ways around this:

- Ask a friend with good handwriting to write it for you.

- Use rubber stamps – there are many stamps available with greetings and messages, which are ideal for when you are making a batch of cards, for instance Christmas cards.

- Use peel-off alphabet or number stickers or rub-on transfers for letters, numbers and phrases – many different styles and colours are available.

- Print a message using a home computer – use regular paper, parchment paper or thin card in the printer. You can also print out onto paper, cut it out and mount on parchment or other decorative paper.

LET'S GET TO WORK!

Put some real bounce into celebrating your soccer star's special day, whether a birthday or a championship win, with this action-packed card. Its dynamic design has been created with simple peel-off stickers and coils of silver wire, to create the impression of the soccer balls in motion. The strong, graphic elements and colour contrast add to the overall impact.

BRIGHT SPARK
YOU COULD CHOOSE THE COLOURS OF THE RECIPIENT'S FAVOURITE SOCCER TEAM AND THEME THE CARD ACCORDINGLY.

1 Stick four peel-off soccer balls onto white card and carefully cut around each one using small scissors. Here, three sizes of ball are used: two large, one medium and one small soccer ball.

2 Using pliers, cut a 12cm (4¾in) length of wire. Using your hands and the natural coil of the wire, twist it to make small loops. Cut one 10cm (4in) and two 8cm (3¼in) lengths and make three more looped pieces in the same way.

YOU WILL NEED white card ■ green card 18 x 23cm (7 x 9in), scored and folded in half, used horizontally ■ dark green card no less than 2 x 18cm (¾ x 7in) ■ light green card 7 x 18cm (2¾ x 7in) ■ soccer ball and soccer player peel-off stickers ■ silver wire, 24 gauge ■ pliers ■ tapestry needle ■ fancy-edged scissors ■ Basic Tool Kit (see page 8)

3 Using adhesive tape, attach one piece of looped wire to the wrong side of each cutout soccer ball.

4 Open out the folded green card and place right side up on a foam pad. Using the tapestry needle, prick a hole in the centre front of the card about 5cm (2in) from one short edge, then prick another hole 1cm (⅜in) below it. Make three more holes about 2.5cm (1in) apart along the centre front of the card. Make three more holes 1cm (⅜in) underneath these so that you have four pairs of holes.

5 Insert the end of one looped wire into the top hole of one pair of holes, then thread it through the lower hole. Secure the end in place on the card with adhesive tape. Trim any excess wire with pliers. Repeat with the other looped wires and pairs of holes.

6 Using fancy-edged scissors, cut along the dark green card 5mm (³⁄₁₆in) away from one long edge. Glue this edged strip along the bottom of the light green card.

7 Choose four soccer player peel-off stickers and position these evenly spaced along the light green card. Using adhesive foam pads, mount this card to cover the taped ends of the wire.

BRIGHT SPARK
A SCORE COULD BE ADDED INSIDE THE SOCCER CARD WITH A PERSONALIZED MESSAGE.

AMERICAN FOOTBALL
Perfect for congratulating a male on a personal achievement, the same bounce effect is used here to illustrate a winning kick, again using coiled silver wire and in this case gold outline peel-off stickers. These were adhered to brown card for the football and coloured in with white pen, and adhered to black card for the boot, with a piece of white card attached for the leg. The boot and leg, with the wire and ball attached, were mounted onto a green single-fold card using adhesive foam pads. A score was made by placing dots of yellow 3-D paint (see Step 6, page 49) on black card, which was then mounted onto gold and black card. Strips of white paper indicate the goal post and a dark green strip, attached to the bottom edge, was created using the edge of a Fiskars® ShapeTemplate™ and ShapeCutter™ tool.

CRICKET

Devoted cricket fans, whether players or spectators, will be bowled over by this all-action image, which, literally, leaps out from the card. But as all true followers of the game appreciate, cricket is not a sport to be rushed – and the same applies to this card! The technique of 3-D découpage is somewhat time consuming, but it is actually quite therapeutic to sit and cut out several copies of an intricate shape. These are then built up in layers, separated by silicone gel, to give dimension to the image. Rubber stamped and coloured cricket bats have been added as a border.

BRIGHT SPARK
YOU COULD MAKE A GIFT TAG BY USING JUST ONE CRICKET BAT SHAPE AND COLOURING IT IN.

BRIGHT SPARK
YOU COULD ADD A CRICKET SCORE TO THE CARD AND PERSONALIZE IT BY INCLUDING AN AGE OR BIRTHDAY DATE.

1 Cut out four complete cricket pictures from the découpage papers, which have repeated identical images. Put one aside for Step 3. Place a small amount of PVA (white) glue on the centre of the wrong side of a cricket picture, then use a small piece of clean scrap card to pull the glue from the centre outwards and over the edges, going over onto the scrap paper. Stick onto white card. Repeat with the other two images and leave to dry. The paper may wrinkle or 'cockle' a little, but this is not a problem with small images. You can place them under a pile of books if you wish to flatten. Spray glue can be used as an alternative, but ensure that the glue is evenly applied all over the image.

2 Using a small pair of scissors, cut out the image of the cricketer, stumps and ball. You will need two cricketers, one set of stumps and three ball shapes. You may find it easier to roughly cut around each shape and then cut each piece out neatly.

YOU WILL NEED cricket découpage papers ■ white card ■ cream single-fold card 15cm (6in) square ■ cricket bat outline stamp ■ light brown inkpad ■ black and brown watercolour pencils ■ silicone gel ■ tweezers with locking device ■ Basic Tool Kit (see page 8)

3 Hold the first cutout cricketer with the tweezers with a locking device, which saves you from continuously having to apply pressure, and apply dots of silicone gel to the wrong side – be sure to work in a well-ventilated room to avoid inhaling any fumes. Place the cutout directly over the cricketer in the complete picture set aside in Step 1. Repeat with the cutout stumps and ball, placing each directly over its counterpart.

4 Mount a second cutout cricketer layer using the same technique. You don't need to wait until the first layer of gel is dry, but you may find it easier and it dries within a few hours. Mount the two remaining cutout cricket balls.

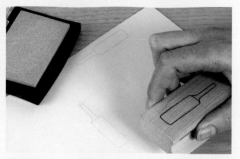

5 Using the light brown inkpad, ink the cricket bat outline stamp and print the image onto the cream single-fold card four times around each edge. You may wish to use a stamp aligner (see page 44) to make sure that the image is central each time, but you can simply line up the stamp by eye.

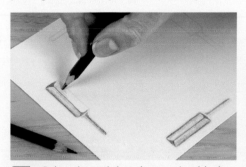

6 Colour in each bat shape using black and brown watercolour pencils. More brown pencil was applied to one side of the bat and more black to the same side of the handle, to give the bat some dimension.

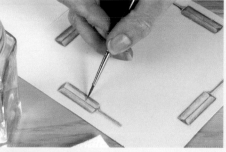

7 Dip the paintbrush into a jar of water and then onto kitchen paper to remove the excess wetness (see Step 4, page 31). Brush over the brown watercolour pencilling with the moist paintbrush to blend the colour. Clean the brush, then repeat with the black watercolour pencilling. Leave the card to dry.

8 Hold the complete cricket image with the tweezers in an old cardboard box, in a well-ventilated room or outside in good weather, and apply spray glue to the wrong side. Position the image centrally on the cream card.

BASEBALL

If he prefers greater swinging action, this alternative 3-D découpage design, with three dynamic players framed by a baseball bat and ball border, will liven up his day. You don't have to use purpose-made découpage papers to create 3-D découpage – you just need multiple identical images. Here, appropriately themed peel-off stickers were mounted onto card and cut out. Two baseballers were glued directly onto the card, while the central figure was raised from the lime green card's surface by using silicone gel. This card square was mounted onto a dark green single-fold card and a red felt-tip pen used to add a stitched effect around the edge. For the border, baseball bat stickers were glued onto white card, cut out and applied in two layers, with the ball applied in a single layer, again using silicone gel.

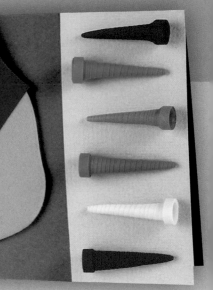

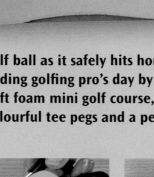

The plop of a golf ball as it safely hits home is music to every golfer's ears, so why not make your budding golfing pro's day by bringing that elusive hole-in-one within easy reach with this craft foam mini golf course, complete with polymer clay golf ball. Quilling is used to make colourful tee pegs and a peel-off sticker golf bag and clubs provides the final flourish.

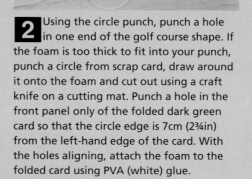

1 Using a pencil, draw a slightly wavy elongated oval shape, about 7 x 15cm (2¾ x 6in) onto the foam, or make a template from scrap card and draw around it. Cut out using medium-sized scissors. Foam is used here for its texture, but you could use bright green paper instead.

2 Using the circle punch, punch a hole in one end of the golf course shape. If the foam is too thick to fit into your punch, punch a circle from scrap card, draw around it onto the foam and cut out using a craft knife on a cutting mat. Punch a hole in the front panel only of the folded dark green card so that the circle edge is 7cm (2¾in) from the left-hand edge of the card. With the holes aligning, attach the foam to the folded card using PVA (white) glue.

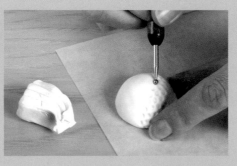

3 Using the palms of your hands, roll a piece of white polymer clay, about 25g (1oz), into a ball shape. Place on a sheet of greaseproof paper and press it down to form a half-ball shape. Press the metal ball of an embossing tool into the clay to make indents. Start from one side and work over to the other side, then continue to cover the whole shape with evenly spaced indents. Polymer clay can leave a greasy residue, so protect your work surface.

YOU WILL NEED dark green card 25 x 18cm (10 x 7in), scored and folded in half, used horizontally ■ black paper 6.5 x 10cm (2½ x 4in), plus extra for strips ■ quilling papers 3mm (⅛in) wide – red, orange, yellow, green and blue ■ two pieces of light green card 9 x 4cm (3½ x 1½in) ■ red card 5cm (2in) square ■ lime green craft foam ■ peel-off number stickers or black pen ■ silver golf bag and clubs peel-off sticker ■ white polymer clay ■ circle punch, 5cm (2in) diameter ■ embossing tool ■ greaseproof paper ■ Basic Tool Kit (see page 8)

4 Transfer the greaseproof paper with the polymer clay ball to a baking tray and bake in an oven according to the manufacturer's instructions. Leave to cool on a wire cooling rack.

5 Glue the black paper rectangle inside the dark green card behind the punched hole, on the unpunched back panel. Using superglue, attach the golf ball to the black paper, making sure that it is positioned so that the punched hole fits over the ball.

BRIGHT SPARK
THE COLOUR OF THE GOLF BALL CAN BE CHANGED TO BRIGHT ORANGE OR YELLOW BY USING DIFFERENT-COLOURED POLYMER CLAY.

6 Cut a 40cm (16in) length of red quilling paper and insert one end through the quilling tool prongs (see page 18). Coil for three turns, keeping the paper taut with your spare hand. Now coil the paper away from the tool, creating a cone shape.

7 Continue coiling away from the tool until the end of the paper is reached. Carefully remove the quilling tool and, using PVA (white) glue, secure the end of the paper in place. Use the cocktail stick to apply a good coating of glue inside the cone shape, right down to the bottom, to give it some rigidity. Make one more red cone, one orange, one yellow, one green and one blue in the same way and glue to one of the pieces of light green card, facing in alternate directions.

8 Cut three 1.5cm (⅝in) lengths of 1cm (⅜in) wide black paper. Wrap one piece around a cocktail stick and glue the end in place to create a band of black. Repeat with the other two pieces at regular intervals along the cocktail stick. Using the template on page 96, cut out a flag from the red card. Use peel-off number stickers or a black pen to add 18 to the flag or a number of your choice. Using PVA (white) glue, attach the flag to the top of the cocktail stick, then the cocktail stick to the card.

9 Attach the silver golf bag and clubs peel-off sticker to the other piece of light green card. Use tweezers to add the three inner peel-off sticker parts to the bag or these could be coloured in using felt-tip pens. Glue this card panel to the left-hand end of the dark green folded card and the other panel with the quilled tee pegs to the other end.

BRIGHT SPARK
MAKE A GOLFING CALENDAR FOR YOUR MAN FEATURING ALL THE MAIN TOURNAMENTS BY DECORATING A BLANK CALENDAR WITH GOLFING STICKERS AND QUILLED TEE PEGS.

FISHING

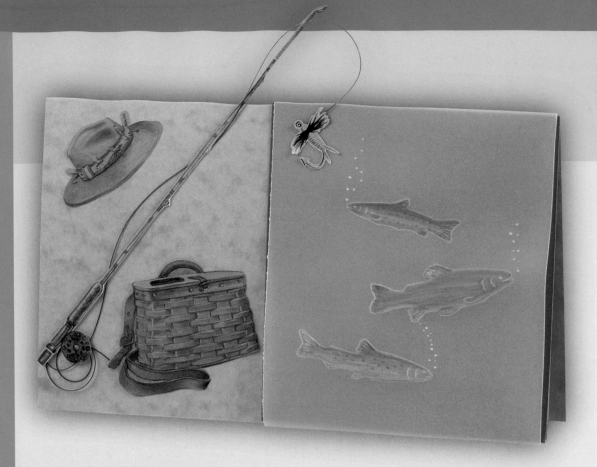

If fishing is your male's beloved pastime, the tranquil, subdued quality of these parchment craft fish in their watery depths will perfectly recall the quiet, contemplative mood of those hours contentedly spent down by the river. The peel-off stickers of the hat, bag and rod denote a fly-fishing theme, but they could easily be adapted for sea fishing.

1 Using a white pencil, trace the three fish outlines from the template on page 96 onto a piece of parchment paper. This is now the right side of the paper.

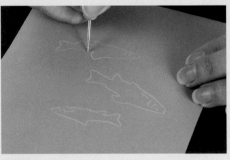

2 Turn the parchment paper over and place on a foam pad. Using the fine ball embossing tool, gently emboss the three fish outlines (see page 19). This is the wrong side of the parchment paper. Turn the paper over to the right side and rub out any white pencil lines with a pencil eraser.

3 Keeping the right side of the parchment paper uppermost, use a selection of watercolour pencils to colour in the three fish. It is best to keep the paper on the foam pad, as the dark colour underneath the parchment paper allows you to see the colours more easily. A selection of greens, yellows and greys was used for the lower fish, oranges, greens and greys for the middle fish and pinks, oranges and greys for the topmost fish.

YOU WILL NEED sheet of parchment paper ■ bright blue card 12 x 11cm (4¾ x 4¼in) ■ turquoise card 20 x 24cm (8 x 9½in), scored and folded in half, used horizontally ■ fishing embossed peel-off stickers ■ fishing wire (optional) ■ watercolour pencils ■ fine and large ball embossing tools ■ Basic Tool Kit (see page 8)

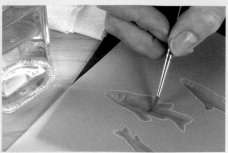

BRIGHT SPARK
IF YOU ARE SHORT OF TIME, USE PEEL-OFF STICKERS OF FISH ON, OR EVEN BEHIND, THE PARCHMENT PAPER INSTEAD OF EMBOSSING AND COLOURING FISH.

4 Dip a fine paintbrush in a jar of clean water, then dab it onto clean kitchen paper, to soak up the excess water but keep it moist enough to use. Too much water on the paintbrush will flood the parchment paper and it will warp or 'cockle'.

5 Using the moist paintbrush, gently blend the watercolour pencilling on each fish. Use the paintbrush in a side-to-side motion to blend along the fish. Clean the paintbrush between each fish by dipping it in the water and then onto the kitchen paper. When finished, leave the parchment paper to dry for a few minutes.

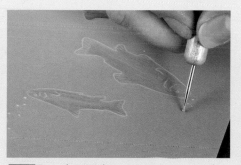

6 Using a dark grey watercolour pencil, add dots of colour to each fish by pressing the pencil onto the parchment paper instead of colouring in as before. Do not press too hard, otherwise the pencil may go through the paper.

7 Turn the parchment paper over so that the wrong side is uppermost on the foam pad. Using the large ball embossing tool, gently emboss the fish bodies. Using the fine ball embossing tool, add bubbles above the mouths of each fish by gently pressing the tool into the parchment paper. Keep checking the right side of the parchment paper to see how the embossing looks.

8 Tear the left-hand side of the parchment paper with a metal ruler (see page 11). Using a craft knife against a metal ruler on a cutting mat, trim the other three edges of the paper so that it measures 15 x 10.5cm (6 x 4¼in).

9 Place a strip of double-sided adhesive tape along the top and bottom edges on the back of the bright blue card. Fold one short edge of the parchment paper over the top of the card and secure to the tape, then repeat with the other short edge on the bottom of the card. Attach two more strips of tape down the sides of the back of the card and attach it to the right-hand side of the folded turquoise card. Attach the hat, bag, fishing rod and fly peel-off stickers to the turquoise card. Real fishing wire was glued to the fishing rod as an authentic touch, but this is optional.

BRIGHT SPARK
IF YOU HAVE A PHOTOGRAPH OF THE FISHERMAN FRIEND YOU ARE GIVING THE CARD TO, THIS COULD BE ATTACHED TO THE LEFT-HAND SIDE OF THE CARD.

BMX

It's a sure thing that the daredevil BMX rider in your life has no fear of flying, forever launching himself into thin air as he jumps from ramp to ramp or flinging himself skywards as he negotiates another bump in the track. So in honour of these thrills and spills, this fun design features a photographic image of a rider on a moving arm, which creates the illusion of the mounted figure flying through the air. The printed base of the card employs a simple 3-D device, but the card will still fold flat for mailing.

1 Take your chosen photograph and place it on a cutting mat. Place the Fiskars® circle ShapeTemplate™, diameter 7.5cm (3in), over the photograph and, using the Fiskars® ShapeCutter™ tool, cut out a circle with the image centred in the circle.

2 Cut another circle the same size from the square of cream card. Apply spray glue to the wrong side of the photograph and attach to the cream card circle.

3 Using a craft knife against a metal ruler on a cutting mat, cut a piece of transparent plastic 12 x 1.5cm (4¾ x ⅝in). Using the point of your craft knife, pierce a small hole in one end of the plastic large enough for the mini brad to pass through.

BRIGHT SPARK
THIS CARD HAS ONE MOVABLE 'ARM', BUT YOU COULD MAKE ANOTHER 'ARM' WITH A GREETING OR BIRTHDAY MESSAGE ON IT.

YOU WILL NEED cream card 11 x 19cm (4¼ x 7½in), plus a piece at least 10cm (4in) square ■ transparent plastic ■ photograph of a BMX rider on a bike (could be from a magazine) ■ toy motorbike ■ silver mini brad ■ black inkpad ■ green felt-tip pen ■ Fiskars® circle ShapeTemplate™ ■ Fiskars® ShapeCutter™ tool ■ mini holepunch ■ Basic Tool Kit (see page 8)

4 Using a pencil, and the template on page 102 if you wish, draw a wavy line across the large piece of cream card. Using the craft knife, cut along the line to create two pieces of card with a wavy edge.

5 Take one wavy-edged piece of cream card and cut inwards 3cm (1⅛in) from the centre of the bottom straight edge and on the other piece the same distance from the centre of the wavy edge, in the position of the dashed lines marked on the template on page 102. Slot these pieces of cream card together to create an 'X' shape.

6 To make the tyre marks, roll the front wheel of the toy motorbike across the black inkpad, then roll it across the cream card, re-inking as necessary. If you cannot find a suitable toy, use a black felt-tip pen to draw the tyre marks.

7 Add marks to the cream card with the green felt-tip pen to resemble clumps of grass, applying the pen in an upwards flicking motion.

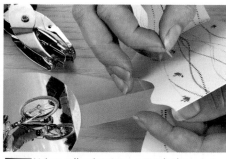

8 Using adhesive tape, attach the photograph to the end of the plastic without the hole. Using the mini holepunch, punch a hole in the cream card where you want the brad to go. Take the silver mini brad and insert it through the cream card and plastic. Flatten the prongs of the brad out on the wrong side.

BRIGHT SPARK
USE THE TOY MOTORBIKE TO PRINT TYRE MARKS ACROSS PLAIN PAPER, AS IN STEP 6, TO MAKE A BACKGROUND PAPER FOR A QUICK BMX CARD.

CYCLING

For those hardy males who prefer the power of the pedal to the motor, this card employs the same 3-D concept as the BMX card, this time in a triumphant finishing-line design. Black and white checked peel-off stickers were placed onto blue card and sticker numbers added for a finishing time. A silver peel-off sticker of a bike was mounted onto a circle of green card and a slot cut top and bottom. This fitted into slots cut in the blue card and green card 'X'-shaped base to allow it to stand up. This finishing line idea could be adapted for a scrapbook page.

BRIGHT SPARK
IF THIS CARD IS FOR A YOUNG SAILOR'S BIRTHDAY, YOU COULD ALSO BUY THEM A BOOK OF KNOTS TO GO WITH IT!

SAILING

Say bon voyage to a seafaring friend or commemorate a sailing success with this smart, shipshape design, complete with a seaman's trusty reef knot, tied through eyelets for a simple yet stylish effect. The gold heat-embossed yacht adds a classy touch and is easy to achieve.

1 Cut around the yacht image on the Magic Motif™ sheet. Remove the clear backing sheet and then place the image in the centre of the square of blue card. Press down and then remove the white front sheet, leaving the transparent image on the blue card. The image will be sticky, so do not touch it at this point.

2 Place the blue card on scrap paper and sprinkle gold embossing powder liberally over the image so that the entire image is covered (see page 17).

YOU WILL NEED blue card 10cm square (4in) ■ pale blue hammer-textured singe-fold card 14.5cm (5¾in) square ■ Magic Motifs™ – 'Sailing' ■ gold embossing powder ■ two 15cm (6in) and two 18cm (7in) lengths of white cord ■ 8 gold eyelets and eyelet setting tools ■ heat gun ■ ceramic tile ■ old cutting mat ■ Basic Tool Kit (see page 8)

3 Hold one edge of the blue card and tip it vertically to shake off the excess embossing powder. Give the card a tap with your spare hand or, if necessary, use a clean, dry paintbrush to remove any powder on the card in areas where you do not want it, taking care not to touch the image.

4 Hold a corner of the card with a wooden clothes peg and hold over a ceramic tile to protect your work surface. Using a heat gun, heat the embossing powder until it melts and becomes semi-liquid. Be careful not to overheat, otherwise the gold will tarnish.

BRIGHT SPARK
IF YOU DON'T HAVE A MAGIC MOTIF™, YOU CAN USE AN EMBOSSING PEN TO DRAW A YACHT SHAPE, OR USE A RUBBER STAMP WITH A SAILING MOTIF AND AN EMBOSSING INKPAD.

5 Place the blue card, right side up, on an old cutting mat and, using the eyelet holepunch and hammer, punch two holes, about 3mm (⅛in) apart, in each corner of the blue card (see page 11).

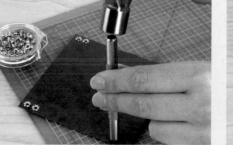

6 Turn the card over, right side down, on the mat and insert a gold eyelet into each hole. Use the eyelet setting tool and hammer to set the eyelets.

7 From the wrong side, insert one shorter length of white cord through an eyelet hole in one corner of the card and then back out through the eyelet hole next to it, so that a loop remains on the side with the gold embossed image.

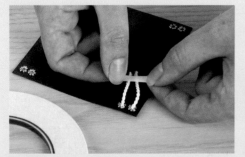

8 Using adhesive tape, secure the ends of the white cord to the wrong side of the card.

9 Thread one longer piece of white cord from the wrong side up through an eyelet and then up through the loop, around the back of the loop, back down through the loop and down through the other eyelet. Using adhesive tape, secure the ends of the cord on the wrong side of the card. Repeat with the other side, ensuring that the knots are staggered. Using adhesive foam pads, mount the card onto the centre of the blue hammer-textured card.

BRIGHT SPARK
THE BOX FOR THE CARD COULD BE DECORATED WITH A KNOT – SEE PAGE 21.

This striking card design is perfect for that aspiring master of the martial arts in your life, whether you want to mark his triumph in a competition or to congratulate him on moving up to the next level of skill. It employs the technique of embossing to make the number 1 on the trophy stand out in relief, and is framed by a border of karate stickers and strips of oriental character printed paper.

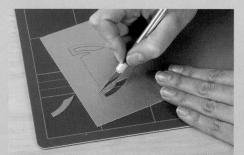

1 Using the template on page 96, cut out a trophy from the gold card with a craft knife on a cutting mat.

2 Place the number stencil, wrong side up, onto the cutting mat and place the gold trophy, wrong side up, on top of the stencil over the number 1. Rub your finger over the trophy to give you an initial outline of the number as a guide and then use the large ball embossing tool to emboss the whole number (see page 19).

YOU WILL NEED gold card 11 x 10cm (4¼ x 4in) ■ red card 15 x 30cm (6 x 12in), scored and folded in half ■ oriental character printed paper ■ karate-themed peel-off stickers ■ number stencil ■ large b embossing tool ■ Basic Tool Kit (see page 8)

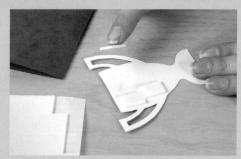

3 Remove the backing paper from several adhesive foam pads and attach them to the reverse side of the trophy, covering the whole area of the card but leaving a 3mm (⅛in) margin around the edge of the trophy.

4 Choose four karate stickers and adhere these across the bottom of the red card, ensuring that they are evenly spaced.

BRIGHT SPARK

TO HELP YOU TO POSITION THE STICKERS EVENLY, ROUGHLY CUT AROUND EACH INDIVIDUAL STICKER FIRST AND TRY OUT THE ARRANGEMENT BEFORE ACTUALLY STICKING THEM DOWN.

5 Cut two strips from the oriental character printed paper 13 x 2.5cm (5 x 1in). Carefully attach these to the top of the red card on the reverse of the front near the outer edges with double-sided adhesive tape.

6 Fold the strips of paper over the top edge of the card, making a crease along the edge. Leave them to hang loose down the front of the card.

GOOD LUCK

The same bold colour scheme as the m card is employed here, and another ready-made stencil, of the Chinese characters for 'lucky', used to create the central motif, but this time heat embossed to produce a raised image (see page 17). The stencil was placed over red card, right side up, and an embossing pen used to colour in the characters. The stencil was removed, gold embossing powder sprinkled over and then heated using an embossing heat gun. The motif was mounted onto oriental character printed card and then mounted onto a red single-fold card.

Often referred to as the sport of kings, given its historic origins, tennis remains a firm sporting favourite with men everywhere, whether of noble birth or not. It makes no difference whether their competitive spirit is fired by actually battling it out on the court or merely by watching the contest unfold. The card of the racket is threaded to produce a convincing strung effect, and the ball is a simple stencil, through which ink is sponged to give a textured look. The brown 'clay' court background could be changed to green for a grass court, in which case make the ball more yellow or white for greater contrast.

1 Using the template on page 96, cut out a tennis racket from the silver card with a craft knife on a cutting mat.

2 Place the silver tennis racket, right side up, on a foam pad. With the needle in the cork, prick evenly spaced holes around the edge.

3 Remove the needle from the cork and thread with the brown thread. Secure the end of the thread to the wrong side of the tennis racket with double-sided adhesive tape. Take the needle out through the first pricked hole at the base of the racket, from the wrong side, and across horizontally to the other side. Take the needle through from the right side of the card, and keeping on this side of the racket, take the needle through the next pricked hole along, then across to the other side. Continue so that all the horizontal threads are complete and secure the end of the thread with double-sided adhesive tape. You may need more than one length of thread.

TENNIS

YOU WILL NEED silver card 20 x 10cm (8 x 4in) ■ burgundy card 5 x 3cm (2 x 1⅛in) ■ black paper strip and white paper strip 3mm (⅛in) wide – quilling paper is ideal ■ cream hammer-textured card ■ terracotta card 21 x 29.5cm (8¼ x 11½in), scored and folded in half, used horizontally ■ brown cotton thread ■ light green inkpad ■ sewing needle set in a dense cork ■ Fiskars® circle ShapeTemplate™ ■ Fiskars® ShapeCutter™ tool ■ sponge ■ Basic Tool Kit (see page 8)

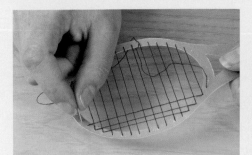

4 Using a new length of brown thread, repeat Step 3, but work vertically this time. You may need more than one length of thread.

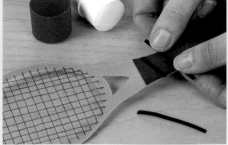

5 Trim the burgundy card to fit the handle of the racket and attach with PVA (white) glue or a glue stick. Cut three 3cm (1⅛in) lengths of black paper strip and glue these diagonally at equal intervals down the handle, ensuring that the ends wrap around to the wrong side.

6 Using the template on page 96, cut out your own tennis ball stencil from scrap card with a craft knife on a cutting mat. Place the stencil on the cream hammer-textured card. Take a piece of clean sponge and dab it onto the inkpad. Holding the stencil firmly in place with your other hand, dab the sponge onto the cream card through the stencil (see page 13). Start sponging around the edges of the stencil first to make them darker. Keep picking up more ink with the sponge and inking the cream card until the whole ball shape is covered. Remove the stencil and leave to dry.

BRIGHT SPARK
IF SHORT OF TIME, CUT THE TENNIS BALL FROM YELLOW CARD INSTEAD OF STENCILLING IT AND DRAW ON THE TENNIS RACKET STRINGS WITH A BLACK PEN.

7 Place the stencilled cream card on a cutting mat. Place the Fiskars® circle ShapeTemplate™ over the top so that the 7.5cm (3in) circle is over the ball. Cut out the ball with the Fiskars® ShapeCutter™ tool.

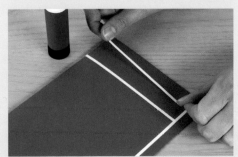

8 Cut two 15cm (6in) lengths of white paper strip and glue to the terracotta card on the right-hand side. Glue the ends of the white paper over the top of the spine of the card. Glue a 19cm (7½in) length across the bottom of the card so that it joins the ends of the other two white strips. Use adhesive foam pads to attach the tennis ball and PVA (white) glue to attach the tennis racket to the card.

SQUASH

The same threading technique is used here on a different racket shape for a squash-lover's card. Use the squash racket template on page 96 and thread it following Steps 2–4. Mark diagonal lines on the handle with a black pen. Glue lengths of 3mm (⅛in) orange paper strip to a 15cm (6in) square single-fold card to resemble the boxes on a squash court. With a circle punch, cut a circle 2.5cm (1in) in diameter from grey card. To personalize the card, a score was added using silver peel-off stickers for the numbers, but any numbers could be used or write a suitable message on the grey ball.

SPORTING LIFE: GALLERY

BOXING *This card really packs a visual punch, with its dynamic 3-D star shape hung with shrink plastic mini boxing gloves – perfect for a rising star of the boxing ring.* Black shrink plastic was cut in the shape of a pair of boxing gloves (template on page 97) and holes punched using a regular office holepunch. It was then heated (see page 46), and the warm plastic moulded around a pencil to create the curved shape. Once cool, thin white cord was threaded through the holes. Two star shapes were cut from red card (template on page 108) and each stamped randomly with a solid star rubber stamp, then heat embossed with gold powder (see page 17). Each star was cut halfway through the centre, one from the top and one from the bottom, and slotted together (see BMX, page 32).

RUNNING *Spur him on to produce his best time in a marathon, or honour him on being the front runner with this medal-winning card.* A yellow single-fold card was decorated by sponging blue running shoe shapes (see page 13; template on page 96). The metal-foil medal was embossed with a running shoe (see page 19), strengthened with two circles of card and red ribbon attached to the reverse. These were attached to the card using double-sided adhesive tape. A bottle peel-off sticker and a stop clock cut from printed paper were mounted onto card and cut out. A running vest was cut from card, details added with a felt-tip pen and peel-off sticker numbers attached. These were mounted using adhesive foam pads.

RUGBY *Give your glutton-for-punishment rugby player more of the same with this real mud- and grass-stained design.* A blue single-fold card was decorated with black and white card to form a rugby shirt shape and embellished with peel-off sticker numbers. The collar was made from a strip of folded card that stands out slightly from the shirt. The mud and grass stains were added last – moist mud (without any stones) was dragged over the surface and the excess shaken off, then fresh, moist grass rubbed over the card.

SWIMMING

For all those males who like to make a splash, this amusing design, simply made with stickers and a foot-shaped punch, is sure to make the right impact. Water droplet stickers were stuck onto a piece of clear rigid plastic to form the shape of a splash. Two feet were punched from pink paper with a foot-shaped punch and a diving board cut from card and attached to the plastic. A blue single-fold card was trimmed so that the front was much lower in height than the back. The plastic was attached to the reverse of the front of the card, then paper with a water design cut and glued to the front. A wavy peel-off sticker was placed across the top of the water paper and also on the back section of the card.

SKATEBOARDING

The design of this card reflects the urban environment skateboarders love, and featuring polymer clay skateboards, it is ideal for teenage boys. The characteristically bright colours of skateboards can be convincingly replicated by mixing polymer clays together. The wheels were made separately and baked alongside the board (see page 28), then attached to the board using superglue. Quilting fabric printed with a brick-style pattern was attached to card, which had already been scored and folded, with double-sided adhesive tape, and the reverse of the card backed with paper. Shapes of grey card were glued to the 'brick' to resemble steps, rails and curves, then the skateboards attached.

HORSERACING

A first-past-the-post design, this 3-D card, which folds flat for mailing, features a steeplechase jump and a trio of jockey colours. Shirts and caps were cut from coloured card and mounted onto green card (templates on page 106). Brown card of the same length but taller was fringed, then a strip of 1cm (³⁄₈in) wide brown quilling paper glued near to the top. A third piece of green card of the same length was cut in a wavy shape. These three pieces of card were attached to two pieces of concertina-folded green card. A finishing post was made from a red circle punched with a 2.5cm (1in) holepunch and a smaller white circle mounted onto it, with brown card for the post.

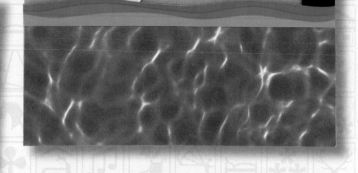

ARTIST

Acknowledge and encourage the artistic endeavours of the aspiring male watercolourist in your life with this appropriately graphic design, with an easel as its centrepiece – the abiding emblem of artists everywhere. The folded style of the card gives due prominence to the easel, complete with colour palette and an experimental daubing of paint, while peel-off stickers and a real wire-bound sketch pad provide your artist with all the other tools of his trade.

BRIGHT SPARK
If short of time, cut out a watercolour picture from a magazine to place on the easel instead of colouring it in.

1 Measure and mark with a pencil on the wrong side of the light blue card 6cm (2⅜in) and 12cm (4¾in) from one short edge – the inner two dashed lines on the template on page 103. Using an empty ballpoint pen or scoring tool against a metal ruler on a cutting mat, score along each line. Turn the card over and repeat 4cm (1½in) and 14cm (5½in) from the short side – the outer two dashed lines on the template.

2 Measure and mark with a pencil 2cm (¾in) and 7cm (2¾in) from the top edge along the inner two score lines. Using a craft knife against a metal ruler on a cutting mat, make two cuts in the card, beginning at these points, following the solid lines marked on the template. Fold the card wrong sides together along the inner two score lines and right sides together along the outer two score lines.

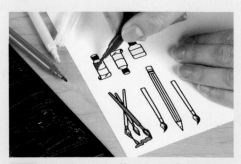

3 Place the peel-off stickers of the group of paintbrushes, pencil, two individual paintbrushes, two tubes of paint and a paint pot on white card. Colour with felt-tip pens.

YOU WILL NEED light blue card 15 x 18cm (6 x 7in) ■ white card about 10 x 21cm (4 x 8¼in) ■ sheet of watercolour paper 300gsm (140lb) ■ black paper strip 3mm (⅛in) and 5mm (³⁄₁₆in) wide ■ grey card 5cm (2in) square ■ blue paper 2.5cm (1in) square, corners rounded ■ artists' materials peel-off stickers ■ clear resin window 2.5cm (1in) square ■ silver wire, 24 gauge ■ felt-tip pens ■ watercolour pencils ■ mini holepunch ■ pliers ■ Basic Tool Kit (see page 8)

4 Using small scissors, cut around each coloured-in sticker. Where the group of brushes has an inner piece of white card that needs to be cut out, make a small cut through the peel-off outline to allow the inner part to be cut out easily. The peel-off sticker will then remain in one piece and when placed on the final card the section that was cut will join up seamlessly.

5 Cut a piece of watercolour paper 5 x 8cm (2 x 3¼in) and, starting with a light blue watercolour pencil at the top right-hand corner, colour a palette down the right-hand side of the paper. Using a green watercolour pencil, draw a squiggle on the top left-hand side. Dip a fine paintbrush into a jar of clean water, then dab the tip onto kitchen paper, to soak up the excess water. Brush over the green pencilling with the moist paintbrush to blend it and create a watercolour effect. The pencilling on the right-hand side was left without blending to give a brighter effect.

6 Using PVA (white glue), attach the watercolour paper to the centre of the blue folded card, in between the cuts. Glue two 9cm (3½in) and one 8cm (3¼in) lengths of 3mm (⅛in) black paper strip to the bottom centre of the watercolour paper. Don't worry if they overlap the bottom edge of the card, as you can trim the ends later. Glue a 4cm (1½in) length of 5mm (³⁄₁₆in) wide black paper strip along the bottom of the watercolour paper, covering the ends of the other three strips. Attach a 1.5cm (⅝in) length of 5mm (³⁄₁₆in) wide black paper strip vertically at the centre top and a 2cm (¾in) length across the bottom of this.

7 Using the template on page 103, cut a water jar from the grey card. Glue the square of blue paper to the jar and attach one of the individual paintbrush peel-off stickers. Place the clear resin window over the paintbrush and blue card to create a water-like effect.

8 Cut four pieces of watercolour paper 4 x 3cm (1½ x 1⅛in). Using the mini holepunch, punch six holes along the top of each piece of card. The row doesn't have to be exactly straight, but you may find it easier to draw a pencil line as a guide for punching the holes.

9 Using pliers, cut a 12cm (4¾in) length of silver wire. Line up the four pieces of card with the punched holes at the top. Thread the wire through the end hole of all four pieces and then loop it over the top and back round through the next hole along. Continue all the way along. Using double-sided adhesive tape, secure the wire ends in place and attach the pad to the blue card. Add a pencil drawing to the pad. Attach the remaining peel-off stickers and water jar to the blue card.

BRIGHT SPARK
A MESSAGE COULD BE WRITTEN ON THE FRONT OF THE SKETCH PAD INSTEAD OF THE DRAWING OR EVEN A HIDDEN MESSAGE ON THE PAGES UNDERNEATH!

WINE

A wine connoisseur will appreciate the time and care taken in handcrafting this card, like the slow maturing of a fine wine – although happily it doesn't take as long to achieve great results in card making! You will be toasting him in style with this inviting glass of red wine, created using simple embossing techniques. A rubber-stamped corner vine motif together with a wine bottle and corkscrew cleverly crafted from paper complete the elegant picture.

BRIGHT SPARK

THE LABEL OF THE BOTTLE COULD BE CUSTOMIZED TO THE FAVOURITE WINE OF THE RECIPIENT BY USING PART OF A REAL WINE LABEL AND ADDING IN THEIR DATE OF BIRTH INSTEAD OF THE YEAR OF THE WINE.

1 Working over a piece of coloured scrap paper, ink the vine stamp with the green inkpad and print the image onto the clear plastic rectangle of the stamp aligner.

2 Position the plastic rectangle with the printed image on the aperture card in the top right-hand corner where you want the final image to be. Take the plastic corner of the stamp aligner and butt it up against the rectangle.

3 Remove the plastic rectangle, ensuring that you don't move either the card or the stamp aligner corner. Using the green inkpad, ink the vine stamp again and print onto the aperture card, using the plastic corner as a guide for positioning the edges of the rubber stamp block.

YOU WILL NEED cream two-fold card 13cm (5in) square with 7.5cm (3in) aperture ■ parchment paper 12cm (4¾in) square ■ burgundy card 12cm (4¾in) square ■ scraps of silver and brown card ■ green card 14 x 6cm (5½ x 2⅜in) ■ scrap of burgundy mulberry paper ■ olive green paper ■ vine corner rubber stamp ■ green and crimson inkpads ■ watercolour pencils ■ gold pen ■ stamp aligner ■ fine and large ball embossing tool ■ kebab stick ■ kitchen foil ■ Basic Tool Kit (see page 8)

4 Press the green inkpad onto kitchen foil so that it leaves a residue of green ink on the foil. Using a fine paintbrush, pick up some of the ink and colour in the vine leaves. When finished, clean the paintbrush thoroughly and dry. Using a green watercolour pencil, colour in the grapes and blend the colour with a damp paintbrush (see Step 7, page 27).

5 Using a white pencil, trace the wine glass template on page 98 onto the parchment paper. Using the fine ball embossing tool, gently emboss the outline (see page 19). Press the crimson inkpad onto a fresh piece of kitchen foil. Using the fine paintbrush, pick up some of the ink and colour in the wine in the glass. Use the large ball embossing tool to emboss the glass.

6 Place double-sided adhesive tape around all four sides of the aperture on the inside (wrong side) of the card. Peel off the backing paper and place the parchment paper, right side down, onto the adhesive tape.

7 Place double-sided adhesive tape around all four edges of the burgundy card and place over the parchment paper. Apply more double-sided adhesive tape to the front of the burgundy card and fold over the left-hand panel of the aperture card so that it sticks to the burgundy card and becomes a single-fold card.

BRIGHT SPARK
THE CORKSCREW IS QUICK TO MAKE AND COULD BE USED TO EMBELLISH A GIFT TAG FOR A BOTTLE OF WINE.

8 For the corkscrew, cut a strip of silver card 7cm x 2mm (2¾ x ³⁄₃₂in) and wind it around the kebab stick to coil it. Cut out a small piece of brown card about 6mm x 3cm (¼ x 1⅛in), round the ends and attach to the coil. Using mini square adhesive foam pads, mount to the bottom right-hand corner of the aperture card. Using the template on page 98, cut a wine bottle from the green card. Using the same template, cut a wine bottle 'sleeve' from burgundy mulberry paper and attach to the top of the bottle, and a label from olive green paper. Add details to the label with gold pen and glue to the bottle, then attach the bottle to the left-hand side of the card.

BEER

The wine design has been adapted here to suit the tastes of an ale man. The beer glass was traced onto parchment paper (template on page 98), and the outline embossed with a fine ball embossing tool and the 'head' with a large ball embossing tool, with additional bubbles embossed below the froth. The cutout glass shape was then attached to a piece of light brown card the same shape minus the froth, applying small dots of glue to the card to avoid the glue showing through the parchment paper. This was mounted onto a rectangle of parchment paper and then inserted into the aperture of a dark brown card. The bottle opener, bottle cap and bottle were cut from silver, gold and brown card respectively (templates on page 98), plus a label from dark brown card, on which details were added in gold pen.

MUSIC

This elegant design with its rich, ornamental gold and black scheme will sound the perfect note with those men who hold classical music dear to their hearts. Traditional in style the card may be, but the central panel, punched and hung from gold wire, is created using a very modern, magical material – shrink plastic – which is rubber-stamped with a treble clef motif and then reduced in size to create a more intricate-looking pattern. The decorative border of musical notations is easily made with gold-edged peel-off stickers.

1 Using the black inkpad, ink the rubber stamp and print the image onto the shrink plastic, pressing the stamp down firmly and removing carefully without smudging the print. Print the image twice more, using the gridlines on a cutting mat as a guide or a stamp aligner (see page 44). Leave to dry – this will take about five hours.

2 Hold the holepunch upside down and slide a corner of the plastic into the holepunch. Position the plastic exactly where you want the hole to be and punch. Repeat for the other three corners.

3 Put the printed shrink plastic onto a sheet of kitchen foil in a baking tray and heat in an oven according to the manufacturer's instructions.

BRIGHT SPARK
INSTEAD OF USING SHRINK PLASTIC, ONE MUSICAL MOTIF STAMPED ONTO CARD WOULD LOOK EFFECTIVE.

YOU WILL NEED gold card 11.5 x 6cm (4½ x 2⅜in) ■ black card 16 x 19cm (6¼ x 7½in), scored and folded in half ■ clear shrink plastic 20 x 10cm (8 x 4in) ■ musical note rubber stamp ■ gold-edged black musical note peel-off stickers ■ gold wire, 24 gauge ■ black solvent inkpad ■ holepunch, 7mm (5⁄16in) diameter ■ kitchen foil ■ clean wooden block ■ pliers ■ tapestry needle ■ Basic Tool Kit (see page 8)

4 When the plastic has shrunk, remove from the oven and place on a wire cooling rack. Immediately place the wooden block on top of the plastic to ensure that it is flat. Leave to cool. The plastic may not be perfectly flat when you remove the block, but this is not a problem.

5 Place the gold card on a foam pad and then the cooled plastic centrally on the card. Using a tapestry needle, prick a hole through each punched hole in the plastic and through the gold card. Then prick a hole just above each hole in the plastic at the top of the panel through the gold card only, and just below at the bottom.

6 Using pliers, cut four 5cm (2in) lengths of gold wire. Take one length of wire and, from the front, thread one end through the holes made in the plastic and gold card, and the other end through the hole in the gold card.

7 Twist the wire ends together on the wrong side and then secure with adhesive tape. Repeat for the other three corners. Using foam adhesive pads, mount the panel onto the black card.

BRIGHT SPARK
USE THE DESIGN AS A GOOD LUCK CARD FOR A MUSIC EXAM BY WRITING AN ENCOURAGING MESSAGE INSIDE.

8 Attach the musical note peel-off stickers to the card around the central panel. With intricate peel-off stickers, there may be small bits of backing that remain stuck to the sticker that you don't want, so carefully remove these with the tapestry needle or craft knife.

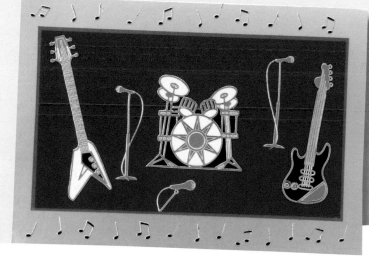

ROCK STAR

Other male friends and family members may well be more in tune with rock music, so play to their rock star dreams with this three-piece band alternative. Centre stage is a drum kit peel-off sticker, which was attached to white card, coloured in with red and black felt-tip pens and then cut out and mounted onto red card. The guitars were added in the same way, together with gold microphones. The red card was mounted onto a slightly larger piece of gold card, then onto a silver folded card. As with the main card, gold-edged black musical note peel-off stickers were used to create a lively patterned border.

This card is a must for a real movie buff, featuring the hallowed symbols of the silver screen – clapperboard, film, audience and even a carton of popcorn! This design majors on the use of apertures, allowing light through to highlight the series of framed images.

BRIGHT SPARK
A BIRTHDAY MESSAGE COULD BE WRITTEN ON THE CLAPPERBOARD OR THE TITLE OF THE RECIPIENT'S FAVOURITE FILM.

1 Place the blue card on a cutting mat and place the Fiskars® square ShapeTemplate™ on top, with the Fiskars® logo uppermost. Line up the grid on the template with the end of the card and the centre score and fold line. Place the Fiskars® ShapeCutter™ tool in the square and pull around the shape with one hand, holding the template down with the other hand. Cut three squares, one 5cm (2in) in the centre and two 3.8cm (1½in) above and below.

2 Roughly cut around the gold rub-on transfer stars, several of each size. Remove the white backing paper from one star and place on the front of the card. Use a teaspoon to press down and rub all over the star, over the transparent top cover. Carefully remove the transparent cover, leaving the star behind on the card. Repeat to cover the front with gold stars.

3 Turn the card over to the wrong side. Place the film negative diagonally across the bottom aperture, trim the ends at an angle so that it fits with a small overlap, then remove. Place double-sided adhesive tape around the edges of each aperture and remove the backing tape. Replace the film negative at an angle across the bottom aperture, then place the parchment paper over all the apertures and press down to adhere.

YOU WILL NEED blue card with white fleck 25 x 15cm (10 x 6in), scored and folded in half ■ parchment paper 23 x 6.5cm (9 x 2½in) ■ black card 10cm (4in) square ■ red striped card 3.5 x 2cm (1⅜ x ¾in) ■ scraps of pale green card ■ burgundy mulberry paper ■ gold rub-on transfer stars, in different sizes ■ piece of scrap 35mm film negative ■ silver mini brad ■ yellow 3-D paint ■ white pen ■ brown felt-tip pen ■ Fiskars® square ShapeTemplate™ ■ Fiskars® ShapeCutter™ tool ■ mini holepunch ■ Basic Tool Kit (see page 8)

4 Cut a piece of black card 2.5 x 3.5cm (1 x 1⅜in). Using a white pen, draw three evenly spaced horizontal lines across it. Add three diagonal white lines across the top. Draw three diagonal white lines in the same position across a piece of black card 1 x 3.5cm (⅜ x 1⅜in), but running in the opposite direction.

5 Using the mini holepunch, punch a hole in the top left-hand corner of the larger piece of black card and in the left-hand end of the smaller piece of black card. From the right side, push the prongs of the mini brad through both holes, from the right side, then bend the prongs outwards on the wrong side, enough to secure it in place but allow the clapperboard to move. Attach to the top aperture with PVA (white) glue.

6 Round the two top corners of the red striped card with scissors. Add a series of small blobs of 3-D paint across the top of the card, to give the effect of popcorn. Leave to dry according to the manufacturer's instructions, but overnight is advisable. Using PVA (white) glue, attach to the blue folded card above the bottom aperture.

BRIGHT SPARK
IF YOU DON'T HAVE TIME FOR THE 3-D PAINT TO DRY, USE SCRUNCHED-UP YELLOW TISSUE PAPER INSTEAD.

7 Cut two small pieces of pale green card, about 8mm x 1.5cm (⁵⁄₁₆ x ⅝in), for tickets. Using small scissors, cut out the corners. Place on scrap paper and, using brown felt-tip pen, draw lines and squiggles to resemble cinema tickets and glue to the blue folded card. Alternatively, you could cut up real (used) cinema tickets instead.

8 Using the template on page 99, cut out the audience silhouette from the remaining black card. Glue to the parchment paper in the middle aperture on the right side. Cut two pieces of burgundy mulberry paper 4 x 6cm (1½ x 2⅜in) and fold concertina-style for curtains. Glue these either side of the silhouette.

PHOTOGRAPHY

If still rather than motion pictures are more your man's focus, then this snapshot design is sure to capture his attention. Again, it features scrap film negative, using two lengths in opposite corners as a basic frame for the design, as well as parchment paper behind an aperture, this time just one in the centre of the blue single-fold card. A silver outline peel-off sticker of a camera was placed onto black card, cut out and then glued to the parchment paper. Two patterned slide frame dome stickers were placed over chosen photographs and then the photos trimmed to size. These were glued over the negatives to hold them in place.

COOKING

Many a young man is now inspired to seek fame and fortune in the kitchen with the advent of the celebrity chef, so what better way to encourage his vocation or applaud his culinary accomplishments than with this composition of a cook's essentials. It features an inventive application of embossing, to give the impression of steam rising from the saucepan. The latter motif as well as the chef's hat offer an additional function, as novelty fridge magnets.

BRIGHT SPARK
ELEMENTS OF THIS CARD COULD BE USED TO MAKE A DINNER PARTY INVITATION OR PLACE NAME CARDS.

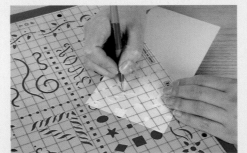

1 Place the embossing stencil in the Fiskars® ShapeBoss™ and peg in place (see page 19). Lift the top layer of the embossing stencil and insert the light blue paper underneath an elongated 'S' shape on the stencil. Using the embossing tool, emboss the paper by pressing down and letting the tool be guided by the template. Then move the paper up slightly and across, and emboss the 'S' shape again. Do this five times to create the appearance of steam, but don't always emboss the whole shape.

2 Remove the paper and trim to measure 6cm (2⅜in) square. Using blue blending chalk and a soft-tip applicator, rub chalk into one side of all the steam embossing to give it definition.

YOU WILL NEED light blue paper 10 x 20cm (4 x 8in) ■ scrap of silver card ■ blue card 19 x 32cm (7½ x 12½in), scored and folded in half, plus two pieces 6.5cm (2½in) and 6cm (2⅜in) square ■ red checked paper ■ white paper ■ floral patterned paper ■ dark blue card 10cm (4in) square ■ 11cm (4¼in) lengths of mid-blue paper strip about 2mm (³⁄₃₂in) wide ■ 2 square magnets ■ mini wooden rolling pin ■ blue blending chalk and soft-tip applicator ■ Fiskars® ShapeBoss™ embossing tray, tool and 'Creative Sampler' stencil set ■ repositional clear adhesive dots ■ Basic Tool Kit (see page 8)

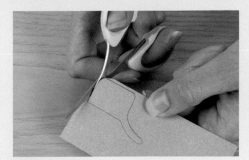

3 Using the template on page 99, cut a saucepan from silver card. Glue this below the steam onto the blue paper. Then mount the blue paper with the saucepan onto the 6.5cm (2½in) square of blue card and then onto red checked paper 3mm (⅛in) larger all round than the blue card.

4 Cut a piece of white paper 9 x 6cm (3½ x 2⅜in). Make six folds across the paper, forming small, equal-sized folds but with larger spaces between each fold, then fold over 5mm (³⁄₁₆in) along one long edge, to create the top of the hat.

5 To make the hat band, cut another piece of white paper 7 x 3cm (2¾ x 1⅛in), fold one long edge to the centre, then fold the other long edge over to meet the fold. Glue the band to the bottom of the hat, wrapping the edges around the back. Mount onto the remaining square of blue card and then onto red checked paper 3mm (⅛in) larger all round than the blue card.

6 Attach double-sided adhesive tape to the back of each magnet. Remove the backing paper and place one on the back of the red checked paper for the saucepan and the other in the same way for the hat.

7 Using the template on page 99, cut out a pair of oven mitts from the patterned paper by placing it printed side down on the work surface and drawing around the template, then turning the template over and drawing around it again before cutting the shapes out.

8 Using the template on page 99, cut an apron from the dark blue card. Place a mid-blue paper strip on scrap paper. Using a cocktail stick, run PVA (white) glue all the way along its length, then place the strip on the apron. Repeat, evenly spacing the strips, across the apron, allowing the ends to overlap the edges. Trim the ends with scissors. Make a loop for the neck from another strip and add two pieces for the waist ties. Cut a pocket from the dark blue card and glue to the apron.

9 Assemble all the elements on the card, except the fridge magnets, and glue in place. Hold the roll of repositional clear adhesive dots in one hand and press one magnet onto a dot to pick it up, then mount onto the card. Repeat with the other magnet. In this way the magnets are easily removed by the recipient and the adhesive dots are thrown away.

BRIGHT SPARK
YOU COULD PERSONALIZE THE CARD BY ADDING FAVOURITE RECIPES OF THE RECIPIENT OR THEME THE CARD ACCORDING TO SEASONAL RECIPES.

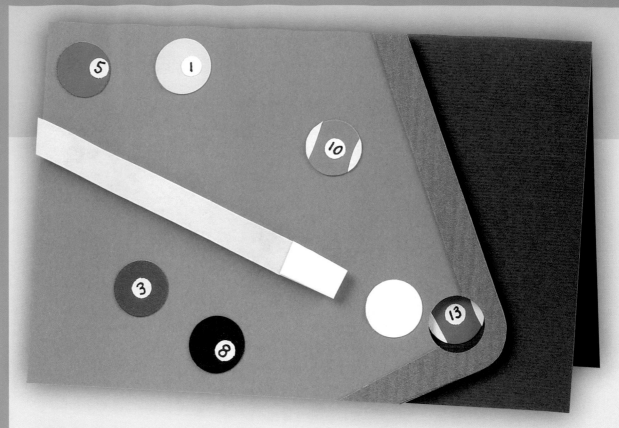

POOL

Many a male is more than happy to wile away his days and nights shooting pool, so this card, capturing some mid-pot action, is sure to find an appreciative audience, whether in celebration of a birthday or perhaps a top score in an exam. This impactful design is quick and easy to create using simple cutout and punched-out shapes.

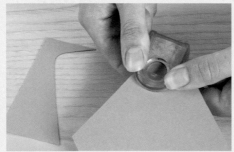

1 Using the template on page 98, cut out a pool table from green card with scissors. Hold the circle punch upside down in the rounded corner where indicated on the template and punch out a circle.

2 Place the pool table shape on the brown card and draw around the top portion, with the rounded corner, and inside the circle.

3 Cut out the top portion with the rounded corner and then punch a circle in the brown card in the same position as in the green card. Cut along the brown card parallel to the edge of the pool table so that you cut through the centre of the circle and continue to the end – you will now have a strip of brown card with a corner in it, in which there is a punched-out half-circle. Using a glue stick or PVA (white) glue, mount this onto the matching section of the green card pool table.

YOU WILL NEED green card 10 x 15cm (4 x 6in) ■ brown card 10 x 7cm (4 x 2¾in) ■ dark green card 15 x 20cm (6 x 8in), scored and folded in half, used horizontally ■ orange, black, white, blue, red, yellow papers ■ scrap of white card ■ cream card 1 x 12cm (⅜ x 4¾in) ■ black fine marker pen ■ circle punch, 1.5cm (⅝in) diameter ■ regular office holepunch ■ Basic Tool Kit (see page 8)

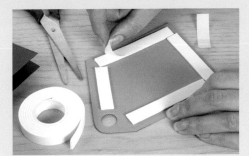

4 Attach strips of adhesive foam pad tape to the back of the pool table. Remove the backing paper and place on the dark green folded card so that the left-hand and top and bottom edges are aligned.

5 Using the circle punch, punch two orange circles, one black, one white, one blue, one red and one yellow from coloured papers. Using the regular office holepunch, punch circles from white paper.

6 Glue a small scrap of white paper to the edges of the blue and one orange circle, then, using scissors and the edge of the circle as a guide, trim off the excess white paper. Glue the small white circles to all the coloured circles except the white one. Using the black marker pen, add numbers to the small white circles as shown.

7 Cut a short length of white card the same width as the cream card and glue to one end of the cream card strip, to form the cue tip. Place a line of mini square adhesive foam pads along the cue and mount diagonally onto the pool table, overlapping the edge slightly. Trim the cue end to align with the card edge. Glue the balls around the cue and one in the hole as if it has just been potted.

BRIGHT SPARK
THE NUMBER ON THE BALL IN THE POCKET COULD BE THE BIRTHDAY AGE OF THE RECIPIENT.

BRIGHT SPARK
IF YOU DON'T HAVE MINI SQUARE ADHESIVE FOAM PADS, SILICONE GEL CAN BE USED INSTEAD OR CLEAR ADHESIVE DOTS.

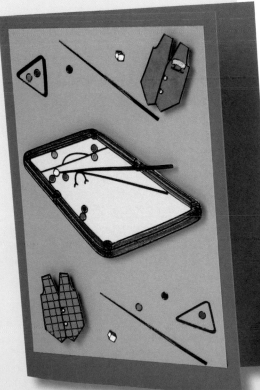

SNOOKER

Every man has his favourite indoor game, and snooker may win out over pool for some, especially since it offers the chance to don a fetching waistcoat! So re-create the glamour and intrigue of a professional snooker match with some appropriately themed peel-off stickers, including the table itself as a focal point, with the edges and balls coloured using felt-tip pens, attached to green baize-like card with adhesive foam pads. This was mounted in turn onto a darker green single-fold card with a glue stick. The two waistcoats were coloured in, cut out and mounted in the same way. The cue, racks and chalk stickers were placed on the green card and coloured in where necessary.

DIY

BRIGHT SPARK
IF YOU DON'T HAVE TIME TO MAKE ALL THE ELEMENTS, THEN USE PRINTED PAPERS FOR ALL THE TOOLS.

A man's shed is a private haven, where many fear to tread unless cordially invited, in which his collection of precious tools takes pride of place. Make him a gift he will truly appreciate, perhaps to congratulate him on his retirement or encourage him to finish that interior makeover, in the form of this gatefold-style card, which opens up to reveal a treasure trove of DIY kit, comprehensive enough to tackle any task. The design makes creative use of printed papers, as well as craft foam, to fashion highly realistic-looking tools.

1 Using the template on page 107, cut out a shed card from the brown card. Measure and mark with an HB pencil the two sets of two dashed lines indicated on the template. Place the card on a cutting mat and, using an empty ballpoint pen or scoring tool against a metal ruler, score along the four lines at the marks.

2 Cut six pieces of cream card: three 10 x 6cm (4 x 2⅜in), two 6 x 4cm (2⅜ x 1½in) and one 10 x 8cm (4 x 3¼in). Using the finished card as a guide, glue these onto the opened-out shed card with PVA (white) glue or a glue stick.

YOU WILL NEED brown card 21 x 28cm (8¼ x 11in) ■ cream card ■ 'Workbench Ephemera' Hot Off The Press™ printed papers ■ silver card 15 x 10cm (6 x 4in) ■ scraps of light and dark brown card ■ craft foam – lime green, red, brown, grey ■ sandpaper ■ 35cm (13¾in) length of fine string ■ pinking shears ■ regular office holepunch ■ Basic Tool Kit (see page 8)

3 Choose which printed motifs you want to use from the printed papers and cut these from the sheet. Here, a measuring tape, set square, nails, screws and numbers were chosen for inside the card. Four hinges were used for the outside of the card, so two packs of the printed papers were used for matching ones. Choose numbers to suit the recipient of the card or you could add a message. Using PVA (white glue) or a glue stick, attach the motifs to the cream panels and the shed card.

4 Using the template on page 107, cut out three chisel handles from lime green craft foam and four screwdriver handles from red craft foam with small scissors – try to use a single fluid cut for a smoother edge. Cut two narrow strips of brown foam 4.5cm (1¾in) and 3.5cm (1⅜in) in length for the hammer handles.

5 Using the templates on page 107, cut one large and one small hammer from silver card. Also cut three strips, about 4cm (1½in) in length, for chisels, then cut four more strips about the same length and trim the corners at one end for screwdrivers.

BRIGHT SPARK
SEVERAL TOOLS ATTACHED TO THE FRONT OF A SINGLE-FOLD CARD WOULD MAKE A GREAT QUICK CARD.

6 Using pinking shears, cut from one short edge into a small rectangle of grey foam, at an angle to the adjacent long edge, to create a saw blade about 7cm (2¾in) in length. Repeat to cut a second blade about 4cm (1½in) in length.

7 To make the saw handles, use a regular office holepunch to punch a hole in light brown card. Move the holepunch along about 2mm (³⁄₃₂in) and punch again. Repeat the move-and-punch process to create an elongated hole. Using the template for the large saw handle on page 107, cut around the hole. Repeat with dark brown card and, using the template on page 107, cut out a small saw handle around the elongated hole.

8 Cut five 2cm (¾in) squares of sandpaper and glue two, overlapping, to the left-hand side of the central part of the shed and four, again overlapping, to the bottom of the right-hand cream door panel. Tie the string in a loop and attach to the bottom right of the central part of the card, then glue all the other elements in place as shown. You can leave a space on the cream card for a message.

▲ *The hinges cut from printed paper and glued to the outside of the card instantly give the impression of a workshed ready to be opened up.*

MANGA

Manga, the hip (Japanese) name for graphic novels, comics and animation, is the medium of preference for many young men, being bold and contemporary in style. Here, it is matched with that other means of communication central to every modern male's existence – the mobile phone – in a scene illustrating it ringing with a birthday message.

1 Photocopy or trace the template on page 99 onto bleedproof marker paper rather than regular paper, if possible, as marker pen bleeds unless used on special paper. Using the fine tip of the flesh marker pen, colour in the boy's face. Start colouring at the outline edge and work inwards.

2 Using the fine tip of the light brown marker pen, colour in the whole of the hair. Take care at the pointed ends of the hair not to go over the edges.

YOU WILL NEED bleedproof marker paper ■ dark orange card 11cm (4¼in) square ■ orange single-fold card 14.5cm (5¾in) square ■ silver number peel-off stickers ■ musical note peel-off stickers ■ dual-tipped permanent marker pens – flesh, light brown, mid-brown, green, grey, yellow, blue, pastel blue ■ guillotine ■ Basic Tool Kit (see page 8)

Use a darker brown marker pen to build up colour in the hair, but don't colour the whole hair – leave some lighter brown highlights showing through. Use the green marker pen to colour in the shirt and grey, yellow and blue for the phone.

4 Using the wider end of the pastel blue marker pen, colour in the background. Colour in large areas of the paper quickly by using long, overlapping strokes of the pen. The edges can be left uneven, as they will be trimmed off.

Using a guillotine or craft knife against a metal ruler on a cutting mat, trim the image to measure 9cm (3½in) square. Using spray glue, mount the image centrally onto the dark orange card, then mount this onto the orange single-fold card.

6 Add the number 15, or appropriate age, in silver peel-off stickers to the screen of the mobile phone. Add musical note peel-off stickers either side of the phone – use a craft knife so that you can pick them up more easily.

BRIGHT SPARK
YOU COULD LEAVE THE CARD UNCOLOURED AND GIVE WITH A SET OF DUAL-TIPPED PERMANENT MARKER PENS AS A GIFT FOR THE RECIPIENT TO COLOUR IN!

BRIGHT SPARK
A BIRTHDAY MESSAGE USING ABBREVIATED TEXT MESSAGING LANGUAGE COULD BE ADDED TO THE SCREEN OF THE MOBILE PHONE INSTEAD OF A NUMBER, SUCH AS 'HPY BTHDAY 2 U'.

COMICS

In contrast to the main card, this design is aimed at an older generation of men, featuring a comic-book graphic that literally depicts the desire to push back time (template on page 99). The figure is shown with a halo of sweat beads, true to comic-book tradition. The same colouring technique has been used as for the manga design. The number can of course be changed to match the male in question's age.

ANTIQUE CLOCK *This elegantly crafted design, enriched with gold embossing 'inlay', is perfect for congratulating those males on joining the ranks of gentleman of leisure, with time on their hands, who have learned to appreciate the fine things in life.* The template on page 99 provides the basic card shape, with the dashed lines indicating cutting lines for the doors. A clear embossing pen was used to draw the inlay, which was then sprinkled with gold embossing powder and heat embossed (see page 17) – you may find it easier to draw and emboss two lines at a time. The clock face is actually a watch face image cut from printed paper. For the chimes, a circle punch was used to cut two circles from gold card and a length of wire inserted in between them before they were glued together. Two rectangles were made in a similar way and all three wires attached to the inside front of the card above the aperture with adhesive tape.

COMPUTERS *Male teens are more often than not glued to their computer screens, so this novelty birthday design, featuring simple cutout card and foam shapes, will require no effort on their part to refocus their otherwise limited attention span!* The main computer components were cut from silver card (templates on page 100) and green craft foam details added. A mouse mat was cut from orange craft foam. Green embroidery thread was taped to the back of each component to resemble wires and then mounted onto orange card, which in turn was mounted onto green and turquoise blue printed card. A corner rounder was used to round the edges to give a softer look. Stickers were used for the numbers on the screen, but you could add a typed message instead.

COWBOYS *Whether the man in your life is a line-dancing ace or a country and western karaoke star, or your lad loves nothing better than to saddle up in his imagination, this printed paper-based design will spur him on to success and pleasure.* For the sheriff's badge, a star (template on page 99) was cut from silver card and a star sticker placed in the centre. A border of holes was then pricked through the card from the wrong side with a needle set in a dense cork. Tight quilled coils (see page 18) of 3mm (⅛in) wide strips of grey paper were added to the tips of the star. The boots, saddle, hat and coffee pot images were cut from printed papers and mounted onto cream card. The hat, lantern and coffee pot were then cut out and the hat mounted onto the card with adhesive foam pads, and wire used to hang the lantern and coffee pot. The fire is made from orange and yellow mulberry paper. A cord lasso adds a final flourish.

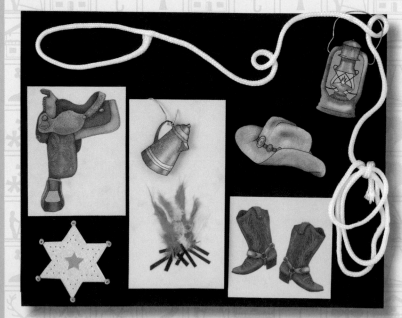

STAMP COLLECTING *Even if avid philatelists do not figure prominently among your male family members or friends, this handsome card featuring a pleasing composition of used stamps from a charity shop could be used to mark a number of occasions, such as a trip abroad or a retirement.* A selection of brightly coloured stamps was made and glued onto yellow card. Some of the stamps were punched using a postage stamp punch, to give them the traditional stamp border. Three special stamps were mounted onto green and then blue card, with clear resin windows placed over the top. The edge of the blue card was cut by using the edge of the stamp punch, by punching a section, then moving the punch along and punching again.

WIZARD *This zany card, created from simple cutout shapes and peel-off stickers, is guaranteed to bewitch your sorcerer's apprentices, or the sorcerer himself, come to that!* Here, an element of manga is used, as the colour of the wizard's face and hand were difficult to find in paper. The face was drawn and coloured in, then mounted onto white card and cut out. Spare cord from the Sailing card on page 34 was unravelled for the hair and glued in place. The cloak, hat and sleeve were cut from dark blue card and small silver peel-off star stickers attached. The shoes were cut from black card and the stick from brown card, then all were mounted onto rainbow paper. The lightning strike shapes were cut from silver paper and glued around the top of the stick (all templates on page 100).

CARD GAMES *You don't have to be a card sharp to love playing cards and card games, so be liberal in dealing out this winning hand, with its unique quilled suit symbols for added 3-D appeal.* A home computer and printer was used to key and print out the A, 2, 3 and 4 onto white card, which were then cut out. Quilled coils using 3mm (⅛in) red and black paper strips were pinched and arranged to form the spade, club, heart and diamond shapes (see page 18). These were then glued in place on the white printed card. A strip of red card was embellished with printed papers and mounted onto the front of a red single-fold card with adhesive foam pads, to form a pocket. The playing cards were then tucked into the pocket, fanned out and glued in place.

PAINTBALLING

This design is for those competitive males who like their action well targeted and colourful, which is just why paintballing hits the spot! The card tells a before and after story, with the card front presenting the teams with their respective coloured balls in orderly fashion at the start of the game, and opens up to reveal a pop-up panorama of splats of colour from the balls as they have exploded on impact.

BRIGHT SPARK
IF YOU CAN'T FIND PRE-PRINTED CAMOUFLAGE PAPER, USE FELT-TIP PENS TO COLOUR YOUR OWN PAPER CAMOUFLAGE-STYLE.

1 Place the sheet of light green mulberry paper on a flat, clean and dry work surface. Dip a finger into a bowl of water and then immediately run it down the mulberry paper in a straight line, about 1.5–2cm (⅝–¾in) from the left-hand short edge. This will wet the paper for about 8cm (3¼in). Dip your finger in the water again and wet the next length, then continue down to the bottom of the paper.

2 With your hands flat on the mulberry paper either side of the wet line, gently tease the paper apart. Because it is handmade it is fibrous, so it will tear in an uneven way, leaving strands of fibres. Make three shorter lengths by wetting across the strip you have just torn. Repeat with the dark green mulberry paper.

YOU WILL NEED sheet of light green and dark green mulberry paper ■ green single-fold card 14.5cm (5¾in) square ■ lime green card 11 x 20cm (4¼ x 8in) ■ orange and pink paper ■ camouflage printed paper 6 x 10cm (2⅜ x 4in) ■ red, yellow and blue card 5cm (2in) square ■ black number peel-off stickers ■ circle punch, 1.5cm (⅝in) diameter ■ Basic Tool Kit (see page 8)

3 Using a glue stick, attach several lengths of dark green and light green mulberry paper horizontally to the front of the green single-fold card, but only to the bottom half of the card. Tear a large piece of dark green mulberry paper about 13 x 26cm (5 x 10¼in) and glue across the inside of the card.

4 Using the template on page 102, cut out the pop-up insert from the lime green card and, using an empty ballpoint pen or scoring tool against a metal ruler, score down the centre line and along the two tabs indicated by the dashed lines on the template, then fold.

5 Using PVA (white) glue, glue one tab onto the mulberry paper-covered inside of the card so that the centre fold of the pop-up is aligned with the centre fold of the card and the tab is angled down from the top edge of the card to the centre fold.

6 Place glue on the other tab, then fold the green card over. Press down firmly on the card and hold for a few seconds for the glue to dry.

7 Using the templates on page 102, cut out two large orange and one large pink splats, and three small orange and two small pink splats from the coloured paper. Using a glue stick, attach these to the inside of the card, over the pop-up and the mulberry paper-covered inside of the card.

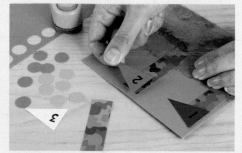

8 Cut three pieces of camouflage paper 9 x 2cm (3½ x ¾in) and three triangles of red, yellow and blue card for the flags. Glue the camouflage poles to the front of the card, with a flag at the top of each, and add peel-off sticker numbers to each flag. Using the circle punch, punch six circles from pink paper and six from orange paper. Glue each set of coloured circles to the card in a pyramid formation.

BRIGHT SPARK
THE SPLATS COULD BE USED TO CREATE AN INVITATION TO A PAINTBALLING PARTY BY PLACING TWO OR THREE ON THE FRONT OF A CARD.

The vegetable patch is traditionally a man's domain, so why not pander to his gardening prowess with this prize-winning bunch of carrots, artfully created using quilling and tied together with real string. Images of gardening gear, cut from printed papers, provide complementary decorative support for the focal element.

BRIGHT SPARK

A DESIGN COMBINING THE BUNCH OF CARROTS WITH A TROPHY (SEE MARTIAL ARTS, PAGE 36) WOULD MAKE A GREAT CONGRATULATIONS CARD FOR A PRIZE-WINNING GARDENER.

1 Cut three 40cm (16in) lengths of orange quilling paper. Take one length and insert into the prongs of the quilling tool (see page 18). Turn the quilling tool around three times, keeping the tension on the paper with your spare hand, then start to coil away from the tool. Continue to coil away from the tool, creating a cone shape.

2 Once you have reached the end of the strip, carefully remove the quilling tool, holding the cone with the other hand. Using a cocktail stick, add a dot of PVA (white) glue to the end of the paper and press into place. Place glue all over the inside of the cone with the cocktail stick and set aside to dry. Make two more cones, but don't try to make them identical – you will never find two carrots the same in real life!

GARDENING

YOU WILL NEED orange quilling paper 3mm (⅛in) wide ■ green quilling paper or paper strips 1cm (⅜in) wide ■ gardening collage printed paper ■ green paper ■ green checked paper ■ light orange card 11 x 21cm (4¼ x 8¼in) ■ dark orange card 21.5 x 23cm (8½ x 9in), scored and folded in half, used horizontally ■ 8 orange and 1 green square brads ■ 20cm (8in) length of string ■ quilling tool ■ mini holepunch ■ Basic Tool Kit (see page 8)

3 Cut nine 5cm (2in) lengths of green quilling paper or strips cut from a sheet of paper. Using small scissors, cut at a 45-degree angle from the edge of one strip to the centre. Continue making cuts close together along each side of the strip, but leave one end uncut. Trim the other end to a point. Repeat with the other strips. Irregular leaves are wanted, so don't be too careful when cutting.

4 Glue the points of three leaves to one end of a 25cm (10in) length of orange quilling paper. Repeat with the remaining leaves. Insert the end with the leaves into the prongs of the quilling tool and start coiling. A flat coil is needed, so do not coil away from the tool this time. Continue until the end is reached and glue the end in place. Repeat for the orange strips attached to the two other groups of leaves.

BRIGHT SPARK
THE CARROTS COULD BE USED TO DECORATE A PHOTO FRAME, NOTEBOOK OR MESSAGE BOARD FOR A FUN YET PRACTICAL GIFT.

5 Glue one tight orange coil with leaves inside a cone. If it does not fit inside the cone shape, try another cone. Because each cone is slightly different, the 'plug' may jut out a little, but this is not a problem.

6 Cut out the gardening gloves and boots from the printed paper. Using spray glue or a glue stick, glue these onto two pieces of green paper 8 x 6cm (3¼ x 2⅜in). Glue a third piece of green paper the same size onto a piece of green checked paper 9 x 7cm (3½ x 2¾in). Attach these three panels to the light orange card, leaving a border around the edge and equal spaces in between.

7 Using an HB pencil, make four pencil marks in each corner of the end two panels and one in towards the top right-hand corner of the centre panel. Using the mini holepunch, punch holes where the pencil marks are.

8 Place an orange brad in each of the four corner holes of one end panel, turn over and bend the prongs outwards to secure in place. Repeat with the other end panel and attach the green brad to the centre panel.

9 Separate each strand of the string and pull one strand away completely. Tie this single strand of string around the middle of the carrots and then wind around the green brad.

2 Place the larger back panel of the card on the upper part of the sheet of parchment paper. Using a white pencil, draw around it across the top, but only partway down the sides to where the front panel joins. Move the template down to align the top with the bottom of your drawn side lines and draw across the top again, so that you have a wavy, sloping line top and bottom. You can use the template you have made, but sometimes in cutting freehand the outline can vary slightly, so use the one you have just cut. Draw around the whole smaller front panel of the card, retaining the straight edge along the bottom. Cut out the two pieces 1cm (⅜in) wider than the card.

Tease your adventure-seeking male with this taste of the wide open snowy slopes and the thrill of a downhill run off-piste. It would make a novel New Year card for an avid skier! Parchment craft is used here to great effect in creating the impression of a snowy landscape, complete with embossed ski runs and punched trees. Ski peel-off stickers and cutout ski poles add the finishing touches.

BRIGHT SPARK
A SCRAPBOOKING-STYLE CARD COULD BE MADE USING A MONTAGE OF SKIING PHOTOS ON THE FRONT AND BACK PANELS OF THE CARD.

SKIING

YOU WILL NEED light blue card 20 x 28cm (8 x 11in) ■ sheet of parchment paper ■ white card large enough for the ski sticker ■ dark blue card 10 x 5cm (4 x 2in) ■ black paper strips 3mm (¹/₈in) wide ■ tree shape fold and punch tool ■ ski peel-off stickers ■ green colouring pencil ■ medium ball embossing tool ■ Basic Tool Kit (see page 8)

BRIGHT SPARK
IF YOU DON'T HAVE A TREE FOLD AND PUNCH TOOL, COLOUR THE TREE SHAPES DIRECTLY ONTO THE PARCHMENT PAPER WITH COLOURING PENCILS.

3 Place the parchment paper for the card back into the tree shape fold and punch tool and punch down. Only half the tree will be cut and a fold line made down the centre. Repeat over the paper, leaving an unpunched area down the centre. Repeat with the other parchment paper, again leaving an unpunched area down the centre.

4 Using the white pencil, draw a faint white line where you want the ski runs to go between the trees on both pieces of parchment paper. Turn the parchment paper over, place on a foam pad and, using the medium ball embossing tool, emboss where you have drawn the lines (see page 19).

5 Place double-sided adhesive tape on either end of the piece of parchment paper for the back of the card and remove the backing tape. Fold the edges of the parchment paper around the straight edges of the card back. Repeat with the other piece of parchment paper on the card front.

6 Lift up the folded part of the punched tree shapes. Colour the blue card inside the punched shape for all the trees with a green colouring pencil.

7 Place the ski peel-off sticker on white card and cut out. Here, they were cut out as a single piece rather than as two separate skis.

8 Using the template on page 109, cut two ski poles from dark blue card. Cut 12cm (4¾in) of black paper strip. Glue one end 1.5cm (⅝in) from one ski pole top. Wrap around the pole, working towards the top. Stop when you have 4cm (1½in) left and glue to the pole top. Glue the loose end to the top for a loop. Repeat with the other pole. Attach the skis and poles to the card.

SNOWBOARDING

Give your fearless snowboarder a sample of the action he knows so well – waving his legs in the air having fallen over yet again – in this alternative parchment craft and sticker design. A snowboard peel-off sticker was mounted onto white card and cut out, then attached to a pair of paper trouser and boot shapes. Parchment paper was embossed with wavy lines (see page 19), a slot cut in it and then wrapped around a card shape similar to the skiing card, also with a slot cut in it. The trouser legs were inserted through the parchment and card slots, then glued. A photo from a skiing holiday was used to provide the landscape backdrop.

BRIGHT SPARK
YOU CAN MAKE OTHER RACING FLAGS, SUCH AS YELLOW FOR DANGER AHEAD, GREEN FOR ALL CLEAR, RED FOR WHEN THE SESSION HAS BEEN STOPPED OR BLUE FOR A DRIVER ABOUT TO BE LAPPED.

FORMULA 1

Fervent followers of Formula 1 racing will be thrilled with this novelty card, which features a magnetic-backed circuit, racing cars and a paper-woven chequered flag – perfect for staging mini F1 races on the fridge while dinner is cooking!

1 Place the two silver racing car peel-off stickers on red and yellow card and the gold racing car peel-off sticker on blue card and cut out with small scissors.

2 Using the smaller circle punch, punch out four circles from black card, leaving a 3cm (1⅛in) space between each one. Insert the black card into the larger circle punch so that the smaller circle is in the centre of the larger punch and punch out. Repeat for the other three circles.

YOU WILL NEED scraps of red, yellow and blue card ■ black card ■ white paper ■ yellow card 11 x 14.5cm (4¼ x 5¾in) ■ red single-fold card 14.5cm (5¾in) square ■ silver and gold peel-off racing car stickers ■ silver pen ■ circle punch, 1.5cm (⅝in) diameter ■ circle punch, 2.8cm (1¹⁄₁₆in) diameter ■ Xyron™ machine and magnetic/laminate cartridge ■ Basic Tool Kit (see page 8)

3 Place the four black tyre shapes on scrap paper and draw on small marks around the outside edge with a silver pen for the tyre tread.

4 Cut eight strips of white paper 5mm x 4cm (³⁄₁₆ x 1½in). Using the template on page 103, cut a flag from black card. Following the dashed lines marked on the template as a guide, cut a fringe in the card ready for weaving.

5 Start by threading one white strip horizontally over the first fringed black length and then under the second fringed length. Continue to the end of the row, alternating over and under the black card. Take another white strip and weave it through the fringed black strips as before, but start by threading under rather than over. You may need to push the white strips together so that there are no large gaps and to create a tight weave.

6 When all the strips are woven, turn the flag over and place adhesive tape around the edges to hold the strips in place.

7 Using the template on page 103, cut out the circuit from black card. Use scissors for the outer edges and a craft knife on a cutting mat to cut the inner part.

BRIGHT SPARK
THIS RACING CIRCUIT IS BASED ON SILVERSTONE IN THE UK, BUT GO TO WWW.FORMULA1.COM TO SEE MANY OTHER CIRCUIT SHAPES ON THE F1 TOUR.

8 Place the three racing cars in the Xyron™ machine with the magnetic/laminate cartridge in. Turn the handle and then insert the flag, turn the handle again and insert the circuit. When the circuit is completely out the other side, cut the strip using the trimmer on the Xyron™ machine.

9 Cut out all the shapes from the magnetic/laminate strip, leaving a 2mm (³⁄₃₂in) border all round. Using a glue stick or PVA (white) glue, attach the rectangle of yellow card to the top of the red single-fold card. Using double-sided adhesive tape, attach the two cars, the circuit and flag to the yellow card – do this by placing the tape on the card first and then put the magnet on top, as the tape doesn't stick easily to the magnet. Glue the tyres overlapping on the bottom right-hand side of the card and attach the last car on the left-hand side.

VINTAGE CARS

1 Using the template on page 109, cut out the double-fold card from the green card. Using an HB pencil, mark on the green card the position of the two score lines marked on the template. Using an empty ballpoint pen or scoring tool against a metal ruler on a cutting mat, score the green card at the marks.

2 Align the template with the bottom edge of the green card and, using an HB pencil, draw around the top of the template, or you may wish to draw freehand. Using a craft knife, cut along the pencil line.

3 Tear a piece of scrap paper in a curve and place this over the lower left-hand section of the green card. Using the brown inkpad, ink the tree stamp and print a row of trees overlapping the scrap paper slightly. The scrap paper is masking the area where the road will go.

If the man in your life is a vintage car owner or enthusiast, or simply has a passion for things from the past, bring him cheer with this nostalgic celebration of the glory days of the early motorcar, pictured paused on the open road winding through countryside under a bright blue sky. In this double-fold card design, the vintage car image has been cut from printed paper and the trees rubber stamped onto the folded flaps.

YOU WILL NEED green card 21 x 27cm (8¼ x 10¾in) ■ blue card 19 x 10cm (7½ x 4in) ■ grey card 20 x 15cm (8 x 6in) ■ vintage car printed paper ■ row of trees rubber stamp ■ brown, green and white inkpads ■ sponge dauber ■ white pen ■ Basic Tool Kit (see page 8)

4 Do not re-ink the stamp but instead, using a piece of kitchen paper, wipe away the ink from two of the tree shapes on the right-hand side of the stamp. Print the trees on the green card above where the first print was made, again overlapping the scrap paper. Using this combination of printing at full strength and masking out, then wiping off the ink and printing, cover the green card on the left-hand and the top of the right-hand side with tree shapes.

5 Place the green card on scrap paper and, using a sponge dauber and a green inkpad, colour in the tree tops with green ink. Intensify the colour of some trees by placing more ink on them and leave some trees lighter. Dab ink over the edges of the green card onto the scrap paper if need be.

6 Place the blue card on scrap paper and drag a corner of the white inkpad over the top of the paper, using twisting and waving motions. You may wish to experiment on a piece of coloured scrap paper first. Continue dragging the inkpad over the paper for a sky effect. Leave to dry. Turn the green card over and fold along the score lines. When dry, glue the blue card to the centre of the green folded card with PVA (white) glue or a glue stick.

7 Using the templates on page 109, cut out a small and large road from grey card. Draw a dashed line down the centre of each road shape with a white pen.

8 Using a glue stick, attach the small road to the left-hand panel and the large road to the right-hand panel. Cut out a vintage car from printed paper and glue to the right-hand panel.

BRIGHT SPARK
YOU COULD MAKE A COORDINATED LINER FOR THE ENVELOPE AT STEPS 4 AND 5 BY RUBBER STAMPING AND INKING A SHEET OF GREEN PAPER IN THE SAME WAY (SEE PAGE **20**).

BRIGHT SPARK
THE VINTAGE CAR COULD BE MADE INTO A MAGNET BY USING A XYRON™ MACHINE – SEE FORMULA **1**, PAGE **67**.

SPORTS CARS

For those men who prefer life in the fast lane, send them this smart, sporty design, which can also be put together with speed by using two of the same sports car silver outline peel-off sticker but facing in different directions and mounted onto contrasting blue card – one light and one dark. They are then cut out and glued onto strips of the contrasting blue card, and mounted onto a red single-fold square card.

WALKING

Nothing could be dearer to the heart of an intrepid walker, rambler or hiker than a good pair of walking boots. So for instant appeal to an adventurous man, in this design the boots form the focal point of a concertina-folded 'landscape' studded with ink-coloured tree cutouts, complete with real laces for an authentic touch.

BRIGHT SPARK

IT IS EASY TO CHANGE THE COLOUR SCHEME OF THIS CARD. FOR EXAMPLE, THE TREES COULD BE IN AUTUMNAL COLOURS BY USING BROWN, ORANGE AND COPPER INKPADS INSTEAD OF THE TWO SHADES OF GREEN.

1 Using an empty ballpoint pen or scoring tool against a metal ruler, score a vertical line on the green card at 10cm (4in) from the left-hand short edge. Turn the card over and score a line 10cm (4in) from what is now the left-hand edge. Fold the card along each score line with the score line inside the fold to make a concertina.

2 Unfold the card and place on a cutting mat. Place the metal ruler at an angle across the card so that it is 21cm (8¼in) from one long edge at one end and 13cm (5in) from the long edge at the other end. Using a craft knife, cut the card all the way along this line.

3 Using the template on page 101, cut out two boots from the brown card with scissors.

YOU WILL NEED green card 21.5 x 30cm (8½ x 12in) ■ brown card 15 x 20cm (6 x 8in) ■ light brown card 15cm (6in) square ■ 8 brass eyelets and eyelet setting tools ■ two 40cm (16in) lengths of brown thonging ■ black and brown felt-tip pens ■ inkpads in two shades of green ■ old cutting mat ■ Basic Tool Kit (see page 8)

BRIGHT SPARK
To save time, the tree shapes could be cut from textured green card rather than coloured with ink.

4 Place the boot shapes on scrap paper. Using the black felt-tip pen, colour in the sole of each boot. Using the brown felt-tip pen, colour in the toe, heel and collar of each boot.

5 Place the boot shapes on an old cutting mat to protect your work surface. Using the eyelet holepunch and hammer, punch four holes for the laces on each boot. Insert an eyelet in each hole. Using the eyelet setting tool and hammer, set each eyelet in place (see page 11).

6 From the right side of the boot, thread 15cm (6in) of one length of thonging through the lowest eyelet and hold in place. Thread the other end of thonging through the next eyelet, again from the right side, and continue with the other eyelets. Tie both ends together in a bow. Repeat for the other boot.

7 Using the template on page 101, cut out ten trees from the light brown card with a craft knife on a cutting mat.

8 Place five tree shapes on a piece of scrap paper. Press the lighter green inkpad onto each tree, avoiding the trunks. Colour the remaining five trees in the same way using the darker green inkpad. When dry, attach all ten tree shapes to the largest two panels of the folded green card using PVA (white) glue. Attach the two boots to the front panel using adhesive foam pads.

HIKING

This alternative card, featuring a trusty backpack, second only to a walker's boots in necessity, uses the same concertina design, but this time with four scored and folded panels and the top cut with a craft knife into irregular mountain shapes. Eyelets were punched in the brown card backpack shape (template on page 101) and blue elasticated cord threaded through. A plastic toggle is used to secure the ends and an old, folded map tucked inside the elastic. The first two panels of the card were coloured in two different greens, then the tips of the mountains with white. Footprint peel-off stickers were added for further dimension.

BRIGHT SPARK
YOU COULD MAKE A BON VOYAGE CARD BY COMBINING THE FLORAL GARLAND WITH AN IMAGE OF A SHIP TIED UP IN DOCK.

Get your jet-setting male in the holiday mood with this composition of classic get-away-from-it-all, chill-out elements – peel-off sticker plane, beach ball and deckchair; inked card and paper cutout palm tree, shorts and Hawaiian shirt; and the traditional 'lei' floral garland, made from tiny punched flowers strung onto thread.

HOLIDAYS

1 Using an empty ballpoint pen or scoring tool against a metal ruler on a cutting mat, score down the blue card 5cm (2in) from the right-hand short edge and fold. Using the template on page 101, cut out a palm tree from the cream card with small scissors.

2 Place the palm tree on scrap paper and, using the small green inkpad, colour in the leaves (see Step 8, page 71). Using a light brown felt-tip pen, colour in the trunk, then use a darker brown to add dashes at the top of the trunk for a palm tree effect.

YOU WILL NEED blue card 16 x 21cm (6¼ x 8¼in) ■ cream card 15 x 10cm (6 x 4in) ■ blue paper 9 x 20cm (3½ x 8in) ■ pink paper ■ scraps of red, white and green card ■ yellow paper 3 x 9cm (1⅛ x 3½in) ■ orange card 10 x 20cm (4 x 8in) ■ palm tree rubber stamp ■ holiday peel-off stickers ■ metal camera charm ■ small flower punch ■ small green inkpad and red inkpad ■ light and mid-brown, blue and red felt-tip pens ■ white pen ■ small sewing needle ■ white and brown cotton thread ■ ribbler ■ Basic Tool Kit (see page 8)

3 Place the blue paper in the ribbler. Turn the handle to draw the paper through and impress a wavy effect on the paper. Cut a section from the ribbled paper, measuring 2 x 9cm (¾ x 3½in), cutting along the line of the wave across the top edge. Keep the remainder for another project.

4 Using the small flower punch, punch out about 60 flowers from pink paper – don't worry, it doesn't take long to punch this number! Work around the edge of the paper, cut off the punched areas in strips, then punch around the edges again. The paper used here is only pink on one side, but this is not essential.

5 Thread the needle with a 40cm (16in) length of white thread and tie a knot in the ends so that it is a double thread. Thread the flowers onto the thread by inserting the needle into the centre of each flower, keeping the pink side facing the same way, if necessary. Tie the ends of the thread together and trim any excess.

6 Using the template on page 101, cut the shorts from red card. Draw a simple pattern all over the shorts with a white pen. Draw a white line across the top of the shorts for a waistband.

7 Place the beach ball and aeroplane peel-off stickers on white card and colour in using felt-tip pens. Cut out the shapes. Place the deckchair onto green card and cut out. Using the template on page 101, cut out the island from yellow paper.

8 Using a red inkpad, ink the palm tree rubber stamp and print onto scrap paper first, then print onto the orange card without re-inking. Print again without re-inking for a fade-out effect. Repeat until the orange paper is printed all along one side.

9 Using the template on page 101, cut out the Hawaiian shirt from the printed card. Mount the palm tree onto the blue card with adhesive foam pads. Glue all the other elements onto the card, with the shirt, 'lei' and shorts on the scored flap. Thread a metal camera charm with brown thread and attach around the shirt neck, securing it with double-sided adhesive tape.

BRIGHT SPARK
SEVERAL HAWAIIAN SHIRTS CAN BE MADE IN ONE GO AND SET ASIDE FOR FUTURE CARDS. ONE SHIRT WOULD BE GREAT ON ITS OWN ON THE FRONT OF A CARD FOR A YOUNG SURFER, WITH A PAIR OF SHORTS AS A FUN GIFT TAG.

STEAM TRAINS

Men and boys alike often have a hankering after the golden age of steam. This card is sure to delight those devotees, with its printed image of a steam engine powering through a tunnel, billowing clouds of steam, which have been given convincing dimension by using puff paint. The inked marks add another realistic touch, bearing testament to the dirtiness of these otherwise majestic machines!

2 Using the template on page 97 and a craft knife against a metal ruler on a cutting mat, cut out the tunnel, aligning the cutout semicircle with the dashed line marked on the template.

1 Using the Fiskars® circle Shape-Template™ and choosing the 7.5cm (3in) diameter circle, cut a semicircular shape from the terracotta card with the Fiskars® ShapeCutter™ tool by making sure that the circle partly overlaps the edge of the card – use the template on page 97 as a guide to positioning the Fiskars® template.

3 Place the terracotta tunnel cutout on one long edge of the blue folded card, with the right-hand edge of the tunnel aligned with that of the blue card. Using an HB pencil, draw around the semicircle onto the blue card. Line up the Fiskars® circle ShapeTemplate™ with the pencil-drawn semicircle on the blue card and cut out.

YOU WILL NEED terracotta card 20cm (8in) square ■ blue card 17 x 20cm (6¾ x 8in), scored and folded in half, used horizontally ■ train printed paper ■ grey card 15cm (6in) square ■ green plastic model foliage ■ black inkpad ■ white puff paint ■ Fiskars® circle ShapeTemplate™ ■ Fiskars® ShapeCutter™ tool ■ hairdryer or heat gun ■ clingfilm ■ ceramic tile ■ Basic Tool Kit (see page 8)

4 Place the terracotta tunnel cutout on scrap paper. Wrap a small piece of clingfilm around your finger, then press it onto the black inkpad. Dab onto the top of the tunnel, starting from the inner edge of the tunnel and dabbing outwards up to the top without re-inking the clingfilm. Dab your finger over the whole tunnel shape, without re-inking.

5 Select your train from the printed paper and cut out. Cut away and discard any steam that may be part of the printed image. Using spray glue or a glue stick, mount the train onto the grey card. Using the template on page 97 and a pencil, draw the outline of the steam onto the grey card. Cut out around the train and steam.

6 Squirt white puff paint onto the area of steam, leaving small gaps of grey card showing through. Leave to dry overnight or follow the manufacturer's instructions for leaving to dry.

BRIGHT SPARK
If you don't have a Fiskars® circle ShapeTemplate™, draw around a tea cup, and if you don't have puff paint, use white 3-D paint or white tissue paper instead.

Using a wooden clothes peg, hold the train over a ceramic tile. Using a hairdryer or heat gun, heat the puff paint, watching closely as the puff paint puffs up, then remove from the heat. If you overheat the puff paint, the white will turn grey, but in this instance it adds to the steam effect.

BRIGHT SPARK
Instead of using green plastic model foliage for the greenery, use cutout paper leaves, green puff paint or rubber-stamped trees

Glue the tunnel to the blue card and glue the train to the tunnel. Glue green plastic model foliage either side of the tunnel.

AEROPLANES

This is an alternative design for those males whose preference is for the glorious flying machines of the past. Puff paint is again used here for the vapour trails of these three classic aeroplanes. The blue background was first inked using a white inkpad to create a soft cloud effect (see Step 6, page 69), then the cutout printed aeroplanes were glued onto the card. The trails of puff paint were added coming from the wing tips and rear of the planes, then heated as in Step 7 of the main card.

BIRD WATCHING

This card offers the budding birder all the essential items of kit for a bird watching expedition, complete with quilled binoculars and craft foam cutout sandwich. A mini notepad was made in the same way as the sketch pad on page 43, with a mini pencil attached. The lenses of the binoculars were made with 5mm (³⁄₁₆in) wide quilling paper (see page 18), coiled to form two long, large cone shapes (see Steps 1 and 2, page 62), then two tight coils made with 3mm (⅛in) wide paper and two eye pieces with 2mm (³⁄₃₂in) wide paper, coiled to form shallow cone shapes, were glued on. The sandwich was made from yellow craft foam pieces coloured with pencils, with greaseproof paper as a wrapper and red checked paper as a napkin. The birds are peel-off stickers mounted onto card and cut out. They were glued to sky patterned paper, which was adhered to a green single-fold card. An old map, cut up and folded, adds a final authentic touch.

MOTORBIKES

Any motorbike enthusiast will be impressed by this spectacle of a succession of rubber-stamped racers dramatically leaning over to take a tight corner. A motorbike was stamped onto light blue card three times with black ink. The bikes were then cut out using the Fiskars® circle ShapeTemplate™ so that each measured 7.5cm (3in) in diameter. The bikes, riders and backgrounds were coloured in using dual-tipped permanent marker pens, as these bleed less than regular felt-tip pens. The three bikes were then mounted onto pre-cut and folded blue card.

CASTLES

Let him know that he really is your knight in shining armour with this stately historical design, featuring a cutout castle archway framing a heroic figure on guard, clutching a gold-embossed 3-D shield. A knight stencil was used as the basis of a simple knight shape, the gaps being pencilled in and a solid shape cut out. It was then coloured in and mounted onto light brown paper. The shield was cut from white card and coloured in using dual-tipped permanent marker pens. 'Gilding' was added around the edge and across the shield using an embossing pen and gold embossing powder (see page 17). It was then mounted onto the knight using adhesive foam pads. An archway was cut in brown mottled card, with darker brown card cut for blocks of stone and placed around the archway. The knight was inserted inside the archway as if guarding the entrance.

TRUCKS *All the lads will love this impressive rig rolling down the open road, simply created using a coloured-in outline sticker.* A silver outline peel-off truck sticker was attached to plain card, coloured in with felt-tip pens and cut out. For the background, the sky effect was creating using a white inkpad on blue card (see Step 6, page 69). Brown and green inks were then sponged onto the lower part for a blurred foliage effect. The road was cut from grey card and a white paper line added to the centre. Dabs of black ink applied with clingfilm (see Step 4, page 75) were added to the road to resemble tyre marks. The truck was then mounted over the top.

SPACE *Transport him to the final frontier with this arrangement of colourful planetary spheres set within a dramatic Lace®-style 3-D design – perfect for a keen student of astrology or science fiction.* A round template was used in same way as for the Christmas card on page 88 to cut half-circles from duo coloured card that is silver on one side and dark blue on the other. Three half-circles were folded over so that the silver side was revealed. The sun was created from orange and yellow mulberry papers, torn to create a feathery edge and glued onto a punched circle, then attached to the centre of the half-circles. The world is a punched circle coloured in with felt-tip pens. The other planets are made from cutout circles coloured with felt-tip pens. A rocket was cut from silver card and mulberry paper added for flames. This card is not accurate for planetary positioning, so if giving it to somebody who is in the know, prepare for a lecture!

FLOWER GARDENING *This quaint potting shed, with its parchment paper window, dainty quilled trowels and flowers, and printed paper paraphernalia, will charm any green-fingered male.* An aperture was cut in the front of a green single-fold card trimmed to a point, and parchment paper mounted behind (see page 48). A cutout butterfly was then attached to one corner of the window. Pots, watering can, ladybird, soil and labels were cut from printed papers and glued to the folded card and light green paper panels. Two trowels were made from brown 3mm (⅛in) wide quilling paper formed into cones (see Steps 1 and 2, page 62) and attached to black card cut into a shield shape. Each red flower comprises four pinched coils (see page 18), glued together and attached to a green paper stem with small leaves, with a brown card tray mounted across the bottom with adhesive foam pads. A tray of seedlings was created by cutting leaf shapes and gluing them to green stalks, with a tray added as before. A bundle of raffia and a tiny cheeky printed snail provide the final fun details.

BRIGHT SPARK
THIS COULD BE ADAPTED FOR A GRANDFATHER BY MAKING TWO DOORS WITH A PHOTOGRAPH OF EACH SUCCESSIVE GENERATION UNDER EACH DOOR.

FATHER'S DAY

As well as being a day for sending love and thanks to a special dad, Father's Day is a celebration of fatherhood in general, and the particular role that fathers play within the family. With this in mind, the symbolic tree of life is the inspiration for this design, which features metal foil embossing for a subtle relief effect, and incorporates a hidden door that opens up to reveal a photo of the next generation in line.

1 Place the metal foil, coloured side down, on a foam pad. Using the roller ball pen and the finished card as a guide, draw leaves and branches onto the foil. Use a steady hand movement for a smoother line. You can photocopy the template on page 97 and place this on top of the foil, then draw over it with the roller ball pen if you wish, but first the template will need to be reversed on a photocopier.

2 Using fancy-edged scissors, cut across the top of the metal foil so that it measures about 18cm (7in) in height. Cut out the section of foil that has not been embossed, so that the remaining piece resembles an 'L' shape. Set the cutout piece to one side for later.

YOU WILL NEED dark blue card 18.5 x 30cm (7⅜ x 12in), scored and folded in half ■ dark blue card 12 x 9cm (4¾ x 3½in) ■ turquoise metal foil ■ two pewter-finish hinges without holes, 2cm (¾in) in length ■ photograph of your choice ■ acid-free photo mounts (optional) ■ roller ball pen ■ fancy-edged scissors ■ Basic Tool Kit (see page 8)

3 Place double-sided adhesive tape on the silver side of the metal foil and then attach it to the front of the dark blue folded card. Leave a small margin at the top. The edges of the foil will overhang the edges of the card. Using regular scissors, trim the side and bottom edges of the metal foil so that it fits the card exactly.

4 Place the spare metal foil from Step 2, coloured side up, on the foam pad. Using the template on page 97 as a guide, emboss five leaves with the roller ball pen.

5 Using small scissors, cut around each leaf. Cut a piece of metal foil about 7cm x 2mm (2¾ x 3/32in) for the stalk.

6 Trim three sides of the piece of dark blue card with the fancy-edged scissors so that it measures 10 x 8cm (4 x 3¼in). Using small pieces of double-sided adhesive tape or superglue, attach the leaves and the stalk to the front. Place double-sided adhesive tape on the back of each wing of the hinges and attach one wing of each hinge to the back of the piece of card, top and bottom of the left-hand edge, and the other wing of each hinge to the folded card. Insert and glue your chosen photograph to the folded card behind the door or use acid-free photo mounts.

NEW DAD

The proud father will treasure this card for years to come, with a portrait of the newborn babe safely tucked away behind ribbon-tied double doors, framed by the same elegant embossed metal foil leaf design as used in the main card. Sixteen leaf shapes were embossed and cut from metal as in the Father's Day card. A piece of light blue card was trimmed with fancy-edged scissors and attached to a single-fold dark blue card. Eight embossed metal foil leaf shapes were attached to the card across the top and bottom. Two doors were made from the blue card and trimmed with fancy-edged scissors top and bottom. Small pewter-finish hinges secure the doors in place. A small hole was punched in each door and ribbon threaded through, then tied in a bow. Two metal plaques of hands and feet were glued to each door front and a baby photo attached behind the doors.

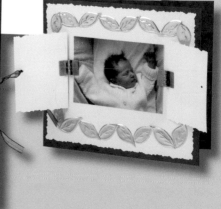

BRIGHT SPARK
FOR A QUICK VERSION OF THIS CARD, JUST MAKE THE HINGED DOOR WITH METAL LEAVES AND ATTACH TO A CARD.

MILESTONE BIRTHDAYS

1 Place the embossing stencil in the Fiskars® ShapeBoss™ and peg in place (see page 19). Lift the top layer of the embossing stencil and insert the yellow card underneath a star shape. Remember that you will be working in reverse, so only emboss the right-hand side of the card. Press the metal ball of the embossing tool around the edge of the shape. You do not need to emboss the centre of the shape.

2 Move the yellow card along, down or around so that you emboss in a different place each time. Chose four shapes – a star, squiggle, line and swirl – and randomly emboss these over the card.

3 Attach the number peel-off stickers to the green card. Using adhesive foam pads, attach the card towards the bottom of the yellow card on the side where the embossing is raised.

Big birthdays aren't always bad news, so send him off on the next stage of life's great adventure with this bright and breezy design. A simple-to-use embossing system creates a textured backdrop for a bevy of colourful quilled balloons, which carry a gift package inscribed with the advanced age of the lucky recipient!

BRIGHT SPARK
IF YOU DON'T HAVE THE 'CREATIVE SAMPLER' EMBOSSING STENCIL SET, YOU CAN USE ELEMENTS OF OTHER STENCILS TO EMBOSS A DESIGN INSTEAD.

YOU WILL NEED yellow card 23 x 18cm (9 x 7in), scored and folded in half ■ green card 5cm (2in) square ■ quilling papers 3mm (⅛in) wide – blue, orange, red, purple, pink ■ small scrap of dark green card ■ green number peel-off stickers 3cm (1⅛in) high ■ silver pen ■ Fiskars® ShapeBoss™ embossing tray, tool and 'Creative Sampler' stencil set ■ quilling tool ■ Basic Tool Kit (see page 8)

4 Glue two 40cm (16in) lengths of blue quilling paper end to end to create a length 80cm (32in) long. Glue strips of orange, red, purple and pink papers end to end in the same way.

5 Place the length of blue paper in between the prongs of the quilling tool and turn the tool around while keeping the tension on the paper with your spare hand (see page 18).

6 Remove the quilling tool, release the coil slightly and glue the end in place so that you have a loose closed coil. Pinch one end of the coil with your fingers to create a teardrop shape.

7 Place PVA (white) glue over one side of the teardrop shape and then attach it to the yellow card. You may need to hold it in place for a few seconds while the glue dries. Repeat for the remaining lengths of coloured paper.

8 Using the silver pen, draw lines from the balloons down to the green card square. Attach the dark green card, trimmed into a tag shape, to the top of the green card square and add a bow in silver pen.

9 Cut a 15cm (6in) length of purple quilling paper and use it to make a loose closed coil. Pinch into a triangle shape. Glue this to the bottom of the purple balloon. Repeat with the other coloured quilling papers and balloons.

70ᵀᴴ BIRTHDAY

Celebrate his big 70 in style with this alternative balloon design, combining an eye-catching printed paper with a sponged and embossed age tag for a suitably sophisticated effect. Number stickers were attached to a square of green paper, then green ink dabbed all over using a sponge dauber. The stickers were then carefully removed to avoid tearing the paper and the outline of 70 was left. The green paper was placed in the embossing system and swirls, stars and shapes were embossed around the number. It was then trimmed and mounted onto blue card and attached to the balloon printed paper, mounted onto a red single-fold card.

21 TODAY

Show your young man that he really has come of age with this refined design, featuring a subtly patterned parchment craft panel sewn onto a printed backdrop, with an additional diamond card attachment framing that coveted 'key of the door' – the traditional symbol of the gateway to adulthood.

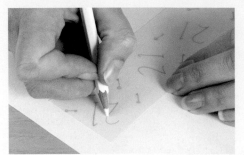

1 Using a white pencil, trace the 21 and key design on page 104 onto the parchment paper.

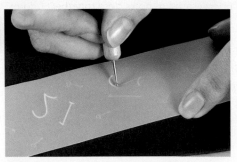

2 Turn the parchment paper over and place on a foam pad. Using a medium ball embossing tool, emboss the number 21s (see page 19) – the numbers will be back to front when embossing.

3 Using a fine ball embossing tool, emboss the key shapes. When finished, turn the paper over and use a pencil eraser to remove any visible white pencil marks.

BRIGHT SPARK
TO SAVE TIME, JUST EMBOSS THE NUMBERS ON THE PARCHMENT PAPER.

YOU WILL NEED parchment paper 17.5 x 5cm (7 x 2in) ■ green patterned paper 17 x 7cm (6¾ x 2¾in) ■ cream single-fold card 17.5 x 8cm (7 x 3¼in) ■ cream card 6cm (2⅜in) square ■ metal key embellishment ■ corner punch ■ medium and fine ball embossing tools ■ sewing needle set in a dense cork ■ sewing needle and green cotton thread ■ Basic Tool Kit (see page 8)

4 Turn the parchment paper over again so that the right side is face down on the foam pad. Using the needle in the cork, prick a series of holes close together to form a wavy line from the bottom to the top of the parchment paper, weaving in and out of the numbers.

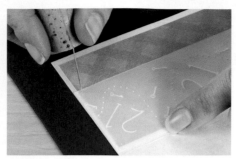

5 Glue the green patterned paper centrally to the cream single-fold card. Open up the single-fold card and place right side up on the foam pad. Place the parchment paper, right side up, to align with the left-hand edge of the card front, covering part of the green patterned paper. Using the needle in the cork, prick 4 holes in each corner through the parchment paper and card.

6 Using the sewing needle and green thread, sew the parchment paper to the card through the holes pricked in each corner, sewing from one opposite corner to another to form an 'X'. Tie the ends of the thread in a knot on the wrong side.

7 Using the corner punch, punch each corner of the cream card square.

8 Secure the end of a 50cm (20in) length of green thread to the wrong side of the card square with adhesive tape. Using the slots punched in the corners of the card, wind the thread around all four sides of the card twice, then secure the other end with adhesive tape on the wrong side. Position the square so that it appears as a diamond. Using superglue, attach the metal key to the centre of the diamond, then attach the diamond to the single-fold card so that it overlaps the edge with PVA (white) glue.

18 TODAY

For many teenage males, turning 18 is actually when they break the chains of childhood, so here's a design that really lets rip in celebration of his manhood, using the parchment craft technique but this time for a fun effect. The number 18 was embossed onto parchment paper, from the wrong side, and, using the large ball embossing tool, dots embossed within the outline numbers. The needle in the cork was then used to prick a random pattern within the number outlines. An aperture was cut in the front of a single-fold card (see page 12) and in a piece of card the same size as the card front, the latter covered with spotted giftwrapping paper. Random cuts were made in the wrapping paper with a craft knife to resemble a gift torn open, and the flaps of torn paper glued in place to keep the aperture open. The parchment paper was mounted behind the aperture and attached to the front of the single-fold card.

VALENTINE'S

Tantalize that special man in your life with this valentine's card with an intriguing twist – let him pull the arrow and he will be greeted with a kiss and a question mark from the woman of mystery! The kiss is quickly created with a rubber stamp, and a decorative border of quilled red hearts adds a further dimension to this heart-winning design.

◀ A secret message of love can replace the question mark, to be revealed only when the lucky recipient pulls the arrow.

1 Using the templates on page 104, cut out the arrow from the pink card and the heart from the red card. Using a white pencil, mark on the heart the position of the four slots indicated by the dashed lines on the template.

2 Using a craft knife against a metal ruler on a cutting mat, cut the four slots in the heart.

3 Insert the pink arrow, point first, into the bottom left-hand slot, then out through the next slot along. Carefully insert it down into the next slot and back up again through the next slot. Pull the arrow right along so that only the tails of the bottom end are showing.

YOU WILL NEED pink card 10 x 15cm (4 x 6in) ■ red card 15cm (6in) square ■ red quilling paper 3mm (⅛in) wide ■ cream single-fold card 14.5cm (5¾in) square ■ lips rubber stamp ■ medium-tip marker or black felt-tip pen ■ pink brush marker ■ quilling tool ■ Basic Tool Kit (see page 8)

4 Using a black marker or felt-tip pen, draw a question mark on the section of arrow showing in the centre of the heart. You may want to mark in pencil where the question mark and lips are to go first to ensure that they are hidden later. Using a pink brush marker, ink the lips rubber stamp.

5 Print the lips on the arrow near the point, but close to the top right-hand slot. When the ink has dried, carefully pull the arrow back through the slots so that the lips and question mark are concealed.

6 Using the quilling tool, make a loose closed coil from a 20cm (8in) length of red quilling paper (see page 18). Remove the quilling tool from the coil and let the coil unwind slightly, then glue the end in place. Make two more coils from 20cm (8in) lengths of quilling paper and three coils from 25cm (10in) lengths.

7 Use your fingers to pinch each coil into a teardrop shape. There will be three slightly larger teardrop shapes, so separate these from the others.

8 Take one larger and one smaller teardrop shape and place glue on one side of each. Then place the shapes next to each other near the bottom of the cream single-fold card on the left-hand side. Hold the shapes in place with your fingers while the glue dries, pinching the bottom of the teardrop shapes. Repeat with the other teardrop shapes so that you have a row of three hearts. Attach the heart and arrow above the quilled hearts, overlapping the top edge of the cream card.

ANNIVERSARY

Move your main man with this powerful symbol of union, the hearts being linked by a twist on the slot technique used in the main card. The same quilled hearts create a decorative frame around the central motif – the amount could match the anniversary. A clever trick gives the arrow the appearance of impossibly passing through two small 5mm (³⁄₁₆in) slots cut in each heart (templates on page 104). However, the arrow was cut 3.5cm (1⅜in) from the arrow tip and the cut end inserted into the slot of the right-hand heart. The other end was threaded through the slot in the left-hand heart and glued to the underside of the right-hand heart. The hearts were mounted onto silver card and then onto slightly larger red card. The panel was then mounted onto the centre of a cream single-fold card. Coils for the hearts were made from 10cm (4in) and 12cm (4¾in) lengths of 3mm (⅛in) wide red quilling paper and attached as for the main card.

BRIGHT SPARK
INSTEAD OF USING QUILLING PAPERS, AN OFFICE SHREDDER CAN BE USED TO MAKE PAPER STRIPS.

NEW HOME

Mark your male friend or family member's relocation in grand style with this imposing 3-D design – a literal interpretation of the age-old saying that 'a man's home is his castle', complete with cord-suspended drawbridge, and cocktail stick and card flag!

1 Using the template on page 105 and a craft knife against a metal ruler on a cutting mat, cut out two large (front and back) and two small (side) castle pieces from brown card. Cut an archway in one larger piece only for the front.

2 Place the castle pieces on scrap paper and colour a line around all the edges with a brown felt-tip pen. Using a ruler, colour vertical lines on each piece, referring to the finished card as a guide. Add short lines for the window slots. Colour both sides of each piece in the same way.

YOU WILL NEED brown card 30 x 20cm (12 x 8in) ■ dark brown card 5.5 x 4.5cm (2¼ x 1¾in) ■ black paper strips 3mm (⅛in) wide ■ scrap of red card ■ brown felt-tip pen ■ 4 dark brown eyelets and eyelet setting tools ■ 30cm (12in) length of cord ■ old cutting mat ■ Basic Tool Kit (see page 8)

3 Place the castle front over an old cutting mat and, using the eyelet holepunch, punch one hole just above the archway on either side, as marked on the template (see page 11). Punch a hole in each corner close to one short edge of the dark brown card.

4 Insert an eyelet in each hole so that the side you are going to hammer is on the wrong side of the card in both cases.

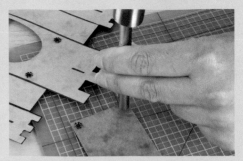

5 Using the eyelet setting tool and hammer, set each eyelet in place.

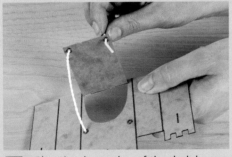

6 Glue the short edge of the dark brown card without the eyelets to the bottom of the card front below the archway. If using thick card, you may need to score a line across the card where it will fold back at the bottom edge of the archway. Thread the cord through the eyelet holes and tie the ends together at the back of the archway so that they are concealed.

7 Cut three black paper strips 3cm (1⅛in) in length and trim one end of each into a point. Glue these across two black paper strips 5cm (2in) in length. Using the template on page 105, cut a flag from red card and glue to the end of a cocktail stick. Using superglue, secure the cocktail stick behind the archway.

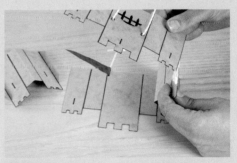

8 Score the castle sides where the dashed lines are marked on the template and fold. Place PVA (white) glue along one of the folded tabs. With the centre fold of the side facing inwards, attach the glued tab to one end of the castle back. Glue the other tab and attach to the castle front. Attach the other side in the same way, with the centre fold facing inwards.

NEW JOB

A new job can be both a daunting and exciting experience, so make sure that he is suitably equipped with this smart 3-D briefcase design, based on the same principle as the New Home card (templates on page 106). Stitching detail was added to the briefcase with felt-tip pen and the handles attached using mini brads (see page 15). A notebook was made in the same way as the sketch pad on page 43, and glued to the inside of the briefcase. The two pencils were made from shrink plastic (see page 46) and a paperclip holding two pieces of green card together adds an authentic office touch. A good luck message could be written on these pieces of card.

This 3-D Christmas card with a difference will not fail to impress any male recipient, although the arty and the techno-minded may be especially appreciative of the Lace® technique, which makes such a striking impact using duo-coloured card. But it can be your secret just how easy it is to achieve!

BRIGHT SPARK
IF YOU ARE SHORT OF TIME, ONE CHRISTMAS TREE WOULD BE EFFECTIVE ENOUGH.

1 Place the duo-coloured card, green side down, on the Lace® cutting mat. Place the Lace® metal template on the right-hand side of the card and fix in place with low-tack adhesive tape. Using the Lace® cutting knife, cut around the outside of the metal template.

2 Flip the metal template over, keeping the centre line in place, and secure in position with low-tack adhesive tape. Place the cutting knife in the outermost slot of the metal template and cut.

YOU WILL NEED sheet of red/green duo-coloured card 21 x 15cm (8¼ x 6in) ■ Lace® tree shape metal template ■ Lace® cutting knife, mat and scoring and folding tool ■ low-tack adhesive tape ■ Basic Tool Kit (see page 8)

3 Cut between all the slots in the template, turning the card with the template attached around so that you are cutting towards you each time.

4 Remove the metal template and low-tack adhesive tape. Cut the corner sections where the knife hasn't quite managed to reach through the metal template. Each tree-shaped section will then only be attached top and bottom to the rest of the card.

BRIGHT SPARK
USE SILVER/BLUE DUO COLOURED CARD AS AN ALTERNATIVE TO THIS TRADITIONAL COLOUR SCHEME. YOU CAN ALSO MAKE YOUR OWN DUO-COLOURED CARD BY GLUING TWO DIFFERENT-COLOURED SHEETS OF PAPER TOGETHER.

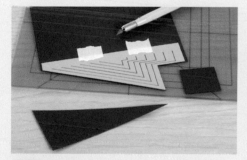

5 Place the template on the left-hand side of the card and secure with low-tack adhesive tape. Cut around the outside of the template and through each slot as before. Remove the template and the low-tack adhesive tape, then cut the corner sections as in Step 4.

6 Place a metal ruler across the base of one set of tree cuts. Using the scoring end of the Lace® scoring and folding tool, score from the top to the bottom of the tree. Repeat with the other cut tree shape.

BRIGHT SPARK
A COMPLETE TREE, CUT OUT AND THREADED WITH A LENGTH OF THREAD THROUGH THE TOP, WOULD MAKE A GREAT CHRISTMAS TREE DECORATION.

7 Lift up the cut sections and, using the folding end of the scoring and folding tool, press the lifted-up sections over to make crisper folds.

8 Place the card on a cutting mat and, using the scoring end of the scoring and folding tool and the gridlines on the cutting mat as a guide, score a vertical line between the two tree shapes.

GRAATION

This design is suitably distinguished to commemorate the academic achievement of a high school or university graduate, featuring a replica of the formal headgear worn for the occasion – the distinctively shaped mortarboard – complete with real handmade tassel. A ribbon-tied scrolled certificate provides an additional ceremonious note.

BRIGHT SPARK
INSTEAD OF USING SCRIPT PAPER, YOU COULD PERSONALIZE THE BACKGROUND BY SCANNING AND PRINTING EXAM CERTIFICATES BELONGING TO THE PERSON FOR WHOM THE CARD IS INTENDED.

1 Using the template on page 104 and a white pencil to draw around the template, cut a mortarboard from black craft foam with a craft knife on a cutting mat.

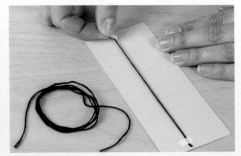

2 Cut a 15cm (6in) length of black embroidery thread. Cut a piece of scrap card 6 x 15cm (2⅜ x 6in). Place the thread across the top of the card and secure to the card at either end with masking tape.

YOU WILL NEED script printed paper ■ burgundy card 21 x 30cm (8¼ x 12in), scored and folded in half, used horizontally ■ sand-coloured paper 8 x 10cm (3¼ x 4in) ■ black craft foam 5 x 19cm (2 x 7½in) ■ black embroidery thread ■ 25cm (10in) length of 7mm (⁵/₁₆in) wide red satin ribbon ■ Basic Tool Kit (see page 8)

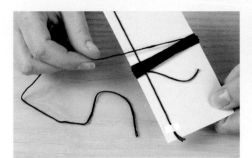

3 Cut a 2.5m (2¾yd) length of black embroidery thread and wind it around the middle of the card.

4 Remove the taped ends of thread from the card and tie tightly in a knot around all the loops of thread wound around the card. Tie a second tight knot to make the first secure. Slide the card out from in between the threads and put to one side.

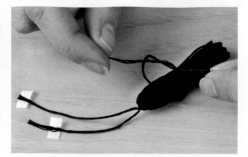

5 Cut another 15cm (6in) length of black embroidery thread and place it under the threads 1cm (⅜in) down from the knot just made. Take either end of this piece of thread and tie a double knot around all the threads. Leave the ends to hang down.

6 Open a pair of scissors and insert one blade in between the looped threads at the opposite end to those tied. Cut through the thread with the scissors. Use the scissors to trim the ends of the threads so that they all hang level.

7 Attach the tassel to the foam hat with adhesive tape. Tear two rectangles of script paper, one about 14 x 20cm (5½ x 8in) and another 8 x 18cm (3¼ x 7in). Glue the larger strip to the burgundy card right side up, then glue the smaller piece right side down on top of the first at an angle.

8 Glue the mortarboard to the card across the right-side-down script paper. Roll up the piece of sand-coloured paper, starting from one short end, and tie the red ribbon in a double knot around the middle to hold in place. Use scissors to trim the ends of the ribbon in a 'V' shape. Use double-sided adhesive tape to attach the scroll to the card below and to the left of the mortarboard and the ribbon to the card.

EXAM SUCCESS

He has to pass a lot of exams before graduating, so this design, featuring a mini envelope bursting with stars on coiled wire, is ideal for celebrating success along the way. It features two torn strips of the script paper glued to a bronze single-fold card. A tiny piece of script paper was glued inside the envelope, which was then glued to the card. Three lengths of silver wire were coiled using pliers and a silver star attached to each end with double-sided adhesive tape. These were glued to the card, the other end inside the envelope. A special message of congratulations could be attached to one of the wire coils.

RETIREMENT

Now that he is retiring, perhaps at long last he'll be able to catch up on all that reading he's been meaning to do but never had the time, or perhaps the man in question is an aspiring writer or keen to write his memoirs. Either way, this elegant collage-style design of book-themed printed images combined with a subtle rubber-stamped background, incorporating a detachable bookmark, will give him all the creative inspiration he needs.

1 Using a cocktail stick, apply PVA (white) glue along the spine only of a gold skeleton leaf and attach to the top of the strip of cream card. Attach a silver skeleton leaf below in the same way. Add one more gold and one more silver leaf to the card to cover it. The ends of the leaves will overlap the edge of the card, but this is not a problem.

2 Cut out a clock, pen, glasses, two closed books and one open book from the printed papers. Glue these to the strip of cream card over the skeleton leaves, with the open book at the top, overlapping the top edge.

YOU WILL NEED cream card 16 x 6cm (6¼ 2⅜in) ■ 'Artsy Collage' Hot Off The Press™ printed papers ■ dark burgundy card 19 x 7cm (7½ x 2¾in) ■ cream single-fold card 18 x 11.5cm (7 x 4½in) ■ gold and silver skeleton leaves ■ clock rubber stamp ■ 15cm (6in) length of 3mm (⅛in) wide gold ribbon ■ cream tassel (ready-made or see page 90 for how to make) ■ dark brown inkpad ■ tapestry needle ■ Xyron™ machine and double-sided laminate cartridge ■ mini holepunch ■ Basic Tool Kit (see page 8)

3 Using small scissors, trim the skeleton leaves so that they are level with the cream card. Trim the cream card around the open book at the top. Using a glue stick, mount the cream card onto the dark burgundy card.

4 Place the card in the Xyron™ machine with a double-sided laminate cartridge and turn the handle to draw the card through and laminate. Continue turning the handle until the whole card has emerged on the other side. Use the cutter on the Xyron™ machine to detach the laminated card.

BRIGHT SPARK
IF YOU DON'T HAVE A XYRON™ MACHINE, A REGULAR OFFICE LAMINATOR MAY WORK, BUT TEST ON SCRAP CARD FIRST.

5 Place the card on a cutting mat and, using a craft knife against a non-slip cork-bottomed metal ruler, trim the excess laminated plastic all round the card.

6 Using a mini holepunch, punch two small holes at the bottom of the bookmark. Thread the ribbon onto a tapestry needle and thread the needle through the punched holes. Thread the needle and ribbon through the loop of the tassel, then remove the needle and tie the ribbon in a bow.

7 Using the inkpad, ink the clock rubber stamp with dark brown ink. If the inkpad is smaller than the stamp, hold the stamp in one hand and press the inkpad onto the stamp. Continue until the stamp is evenly covered with ink.

8 Print the stamp onto scrap paper and then print onto the cream single-fold card without re-inking. Now print again without re-inking to create a fading-out effect. Continue until the cream card is covered with softly printed clocks.

9 Attach silver and gold skeleton leaves to the single-fold card, applying glue to the spine as before. Using a small strip of double-sided adhesive tape, attach the finished bookmark to the single-fold card at an angle.

BRIGHT SPARK
A MESSAGE SUCH AS 'HAPPY RETIREMENT' COULD BE WRITTEN ON THE BOOKMARK BEFORE LAMINATING.

DRIVING TEST *Send him encouragement for the big day or heartfelt congratulations on his success with this quirky multi-element, 3-D design as a memorable memento of a major milestone.* Orange card was scored and folded in a similar way to the Artist card on page 42. An outline peel-off sticker of a car was attached to red card and cut out, then mounted onto orange and red card, with a clear resin window placed over the top. A rubber stamp of car keys was printed onto an orange disk and coloured in. The road map was formed from real maps cut into small squares and glued to a hinged cover. A paper road makes a fun, defining border for the base of the card and the white arrows on the punched blue circles point in different directions to bring movement to the design. The mini clipboard with a red tick indicating a pass adds the finishing touch.

CHRISTMAS *Bring the man in your life some cutting-edge festive cheer with this contemporary take on a traditional Christmas motif, using a single stamp to create mini plastic holly decorations and a contrasting printed backdrop.* A holly stamp was inked with a green permanent waterproof dye-based inkpad and printed onto pre-sanded white shrink plastic on the rough side. A sponge dauber was used to dab green ink around the edge and lightly within the leaf shapes – as the colour intensifies when the plastic is heated, the dauber was only inked once and used to colour all four sprigs. The berries were coloured in using red brush marker suitable for shrink plastic, then the sprigs cut out with a border and heated using a heat gun. Red card was printed with the same holly stamp, the edges inked with the sponge dauber and the berries coloured in. The printed panel was then torn out and glued to a green single-fold card. The shrink plastic holly sprigs were superglued to a torn strip of green parchment paper, which was then attached to the torn red card by placing superglue under the holly only.

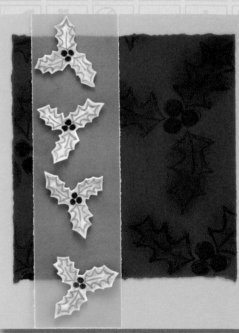

GOOD LUCK *Another age-old symbol is given a fresh, graphic treatment in this single-colour design, featuring a quilled four-leaf clover, set within a masked and sponged frame – the perfect talisman for those males in need of a boost in fortune.* Torn scrap paper and sponged green ink was used to create a border around the edge of this square light green single-fold card (see page 13). The scrap paper was then moved inwards and the sponging repeated so that only a small area of green card was left in the centre. Eight teardrop-shaped coils were made from 40cm (16in) lengths of green 3mm (⅛in) wide quilling paper (see page 18), then glued in a four-leaf clover arrangement in the centre of the card, around a small central coil with a paper stalk attached.

GET WELL *This jolly wiggly-eyed flower, fashioned from quilled teardrop shapes, is guaranteed to bring light relief to any ailing individual – even a male!* Five quilled teardrop shapes (see page 18) were glued to torn orange paper and a punched circle with wiggly eyes and a hand-drawn mouth attached to the centre. A green paper stalk and a small green teardrop-shaped coil for a leaf were then added. A box shape was cut from green card and part of a real (clean!) tissue glued to it, which was then mounted to the yellow card with adhesive foam pads. The first-aid box and thermometer were simply cut from scraps of card, with detail added to the thermometer in black pen.

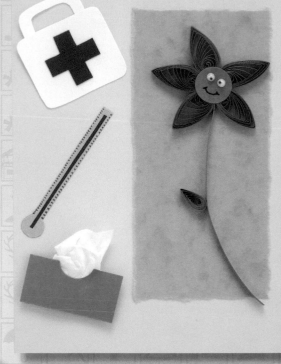

THANKSGIVING *Doubly tempt his tastebuds with this realistically rendered mouthwatering duo of plump roasted turkey – the very epitome of Thanksgiving – and ruby red wine.* The unmistakable cutout turkey shape (templates on page 105) was convincingly coloured using brown ink and clingfilm – see Step 4, page 75. Tight red quilled coils (see page 18) and cutout green leaves were used to adorn the turkey plate. The wine bottle and glass of wine were created in the same way as for the Wine card on page 44. This design could alternatively be used for a Christmas meal invitation.

FOURTH OF JULY *Make the celebrations really go with a bang for your male pals or your nearest and dearest with this firecracker of a design, complete with mini card rockets with coiled paper streamers and kebab stick American flag.* A piece of fireworks printed paper was used for the background, and a decorative border of punched white stars added to the bottom of the card on the front panel and wider back panel. The flag was made from paper and attached to a trimmed-down kebab stick. The card rockets were glued to cocktail sticks (template on page 105), and strips of coiled red paper added to the ends (see Step 8, page 45). Small pieces of the printed fireworks paper were used to decorate the rockets. To adapt this card for a fireworks party invitation, simply exclude the flag.

TEMPLATES

ALL TEMPLATES SHOWN FULL SIZE, EXCEPT ON PAGES 108–109

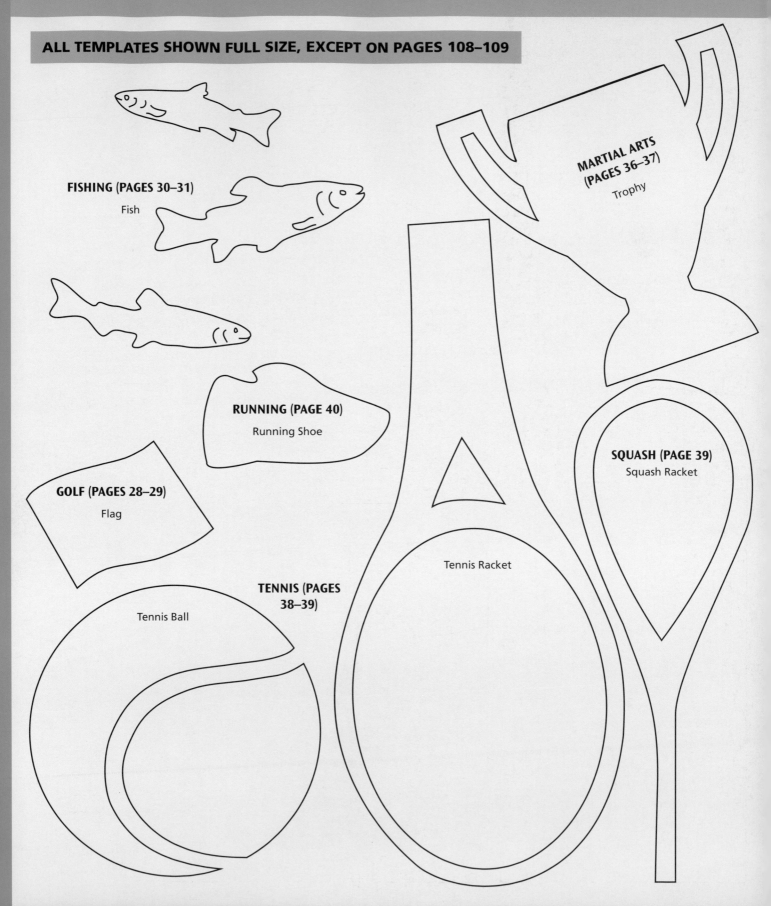

FISHING (PAGES 30–31)

Fish

MARTIAL ARTS (PAGES 36–37)

Trophy

RUNNING (PAGE 40)

Running Shoe

SQUASH (PAGE 39)

Squash Racket

GOLF (PAGES 28–29)

Flag

TENNIS (PAGES 38–39)

Tennis Ball

Tennis Racket

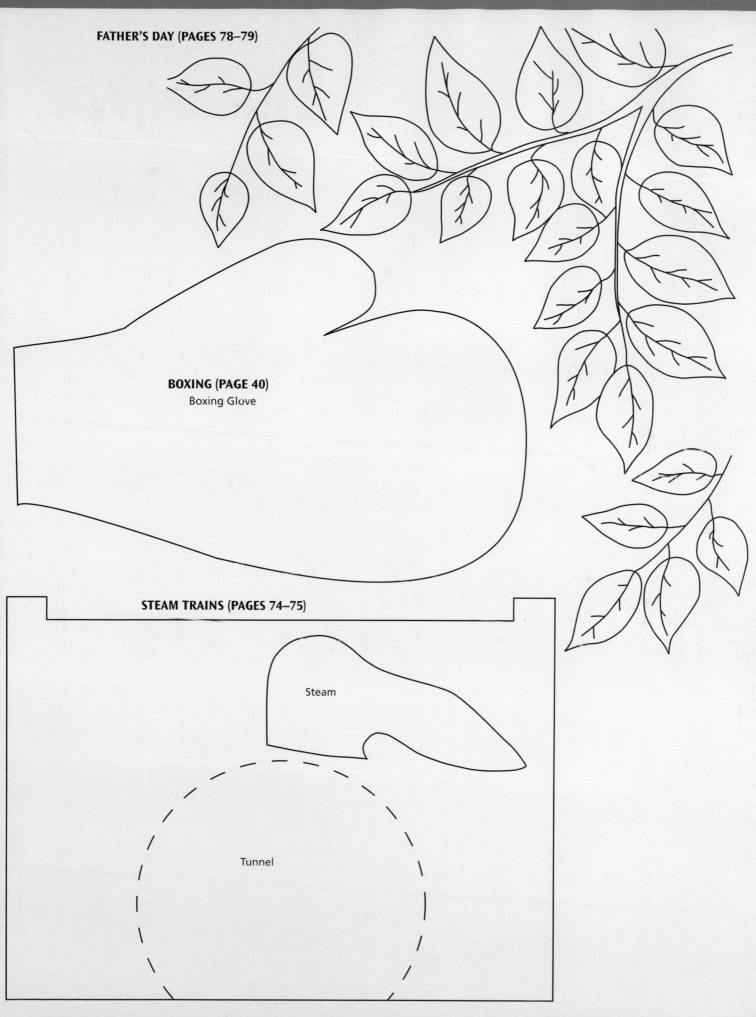

FATHER'S DAY (PAGES 78–79)

BOXING (PAGE 40)
Boxing Glove

STEAM TRAINS (PAGES 74–75)

Steam

Tunnel

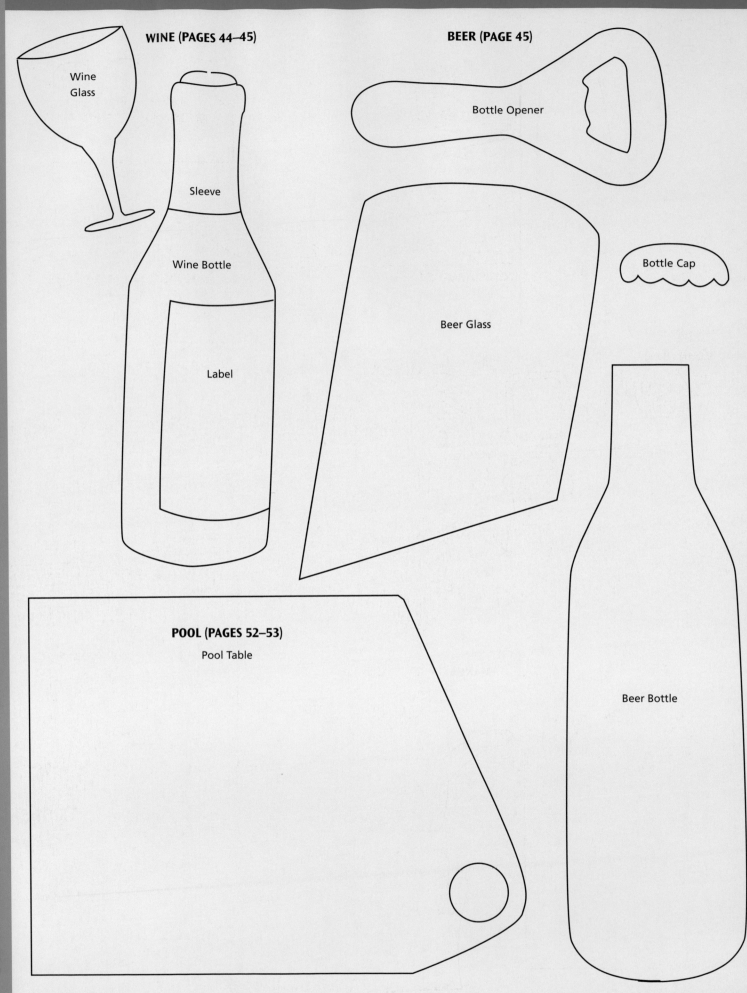

WINE (PAGES 44–45)

Wine Glass

Sleeve

Wine Bottle

Label

BEER (PAGE 45)

Bottle Opener

Bottle Cap

Beer Glass

Beer Bottle

POOL (PAGES 52–53)

Pool Table

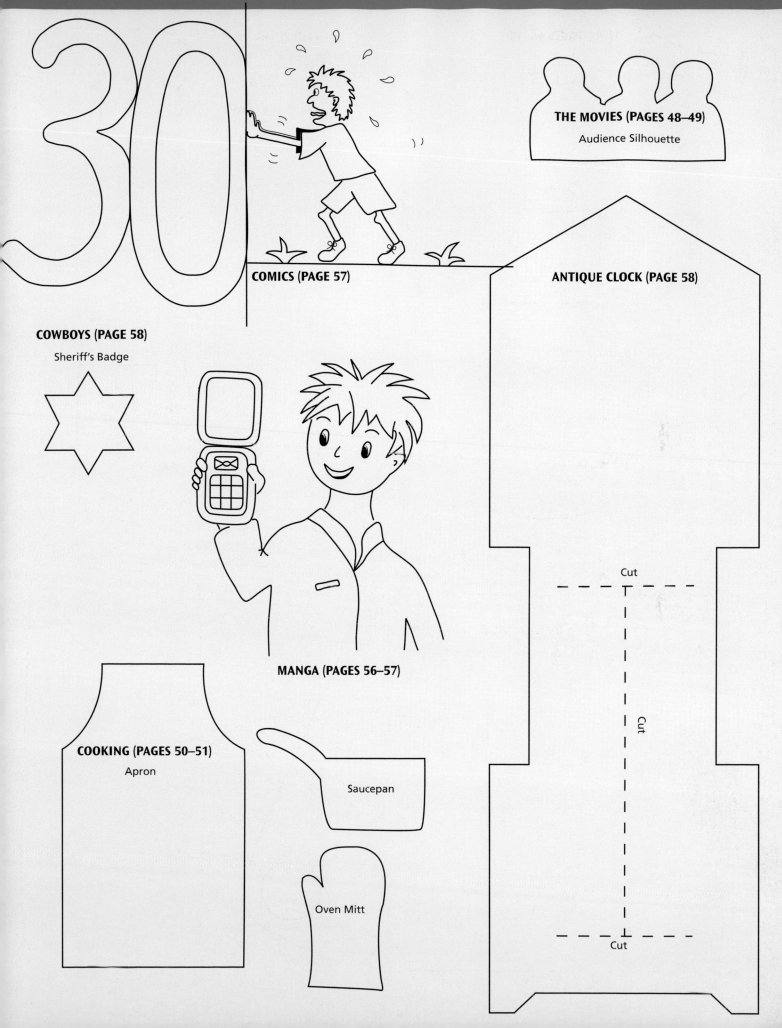

COMICS (PAGE 57)

THE MOVIES (PAGES 48–49)

Audience Silhouette

COWBOYS (PAGE 58)

Sheriff's Badge

ANTIQUE CLOCK (PAGE 58)

Cut

Cut

Cut

MANGA (PAGES 56–57)

COOKING (PAGES 50–51)

Apron

Saucepan

Oven Mitt

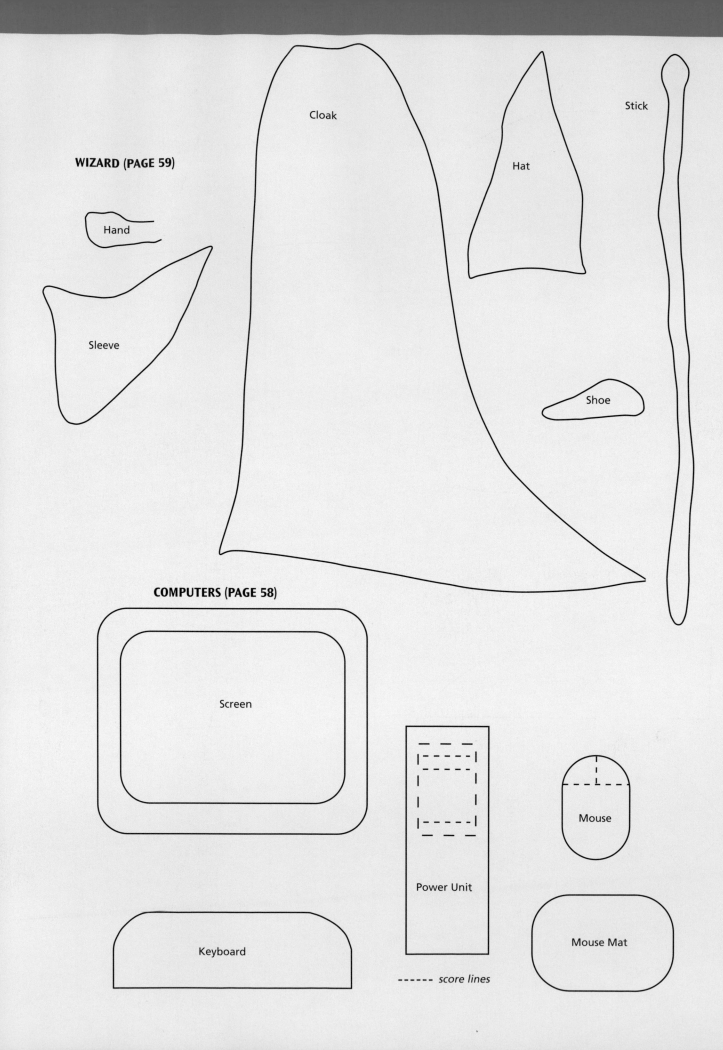

WIZARD (PAGE 59)

Hand

Sleeve

Cloak

Hat

Stick

Shoe

COMPUTERS (PAGE 58)

Screen

Power Unit

Mouse

Keyboard

Mouse Mat

- - - - - - *score lines*

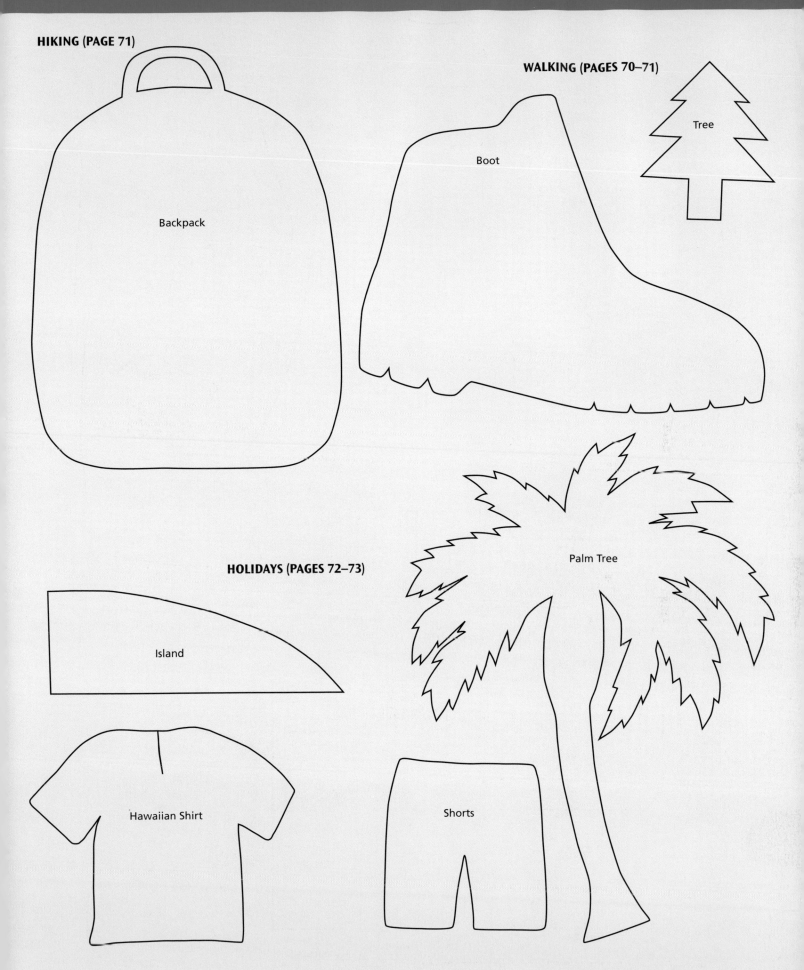

HIKING (PAGE 71)

Backpack

WALKING (PAGES 70–71)

Boot

Tree

Palm Tree

HOLIDAYS (PAGES 72–73)

Island

Hawaiian Shirt

Shorts

Score

Score

PAINTBALLING (PAGES 60–61)

Pop-up Insert

Score

Large Splat

Small Splat

BMX (PAGES 32–33)

Cut

Cut

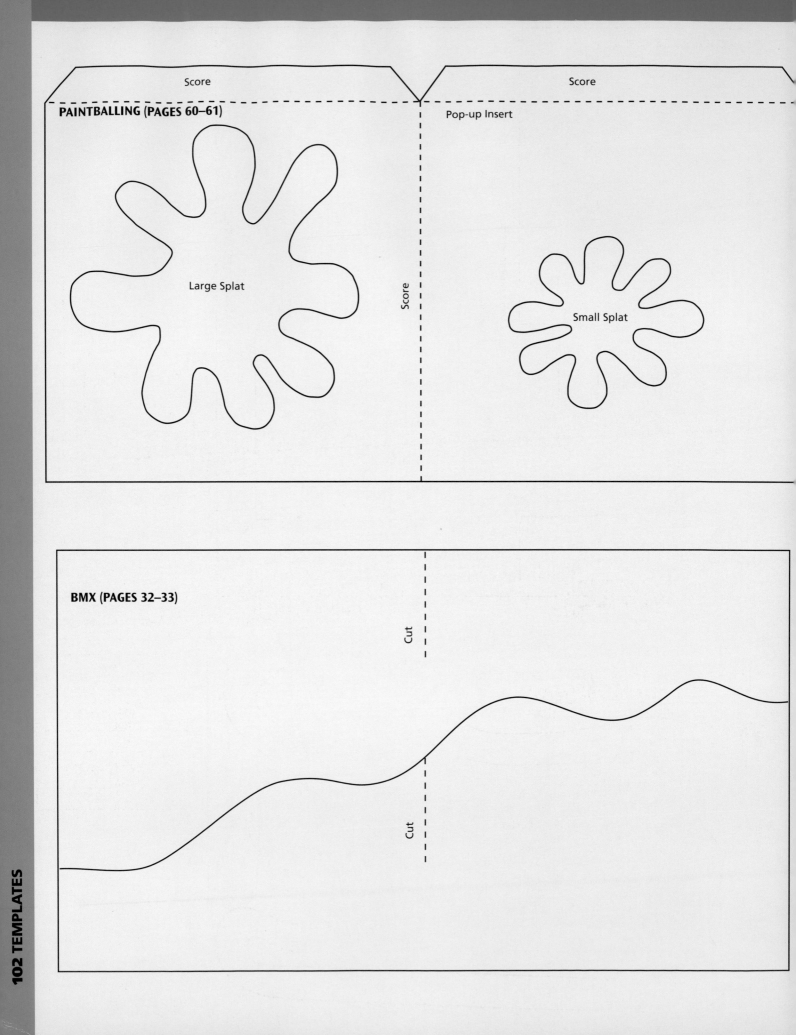

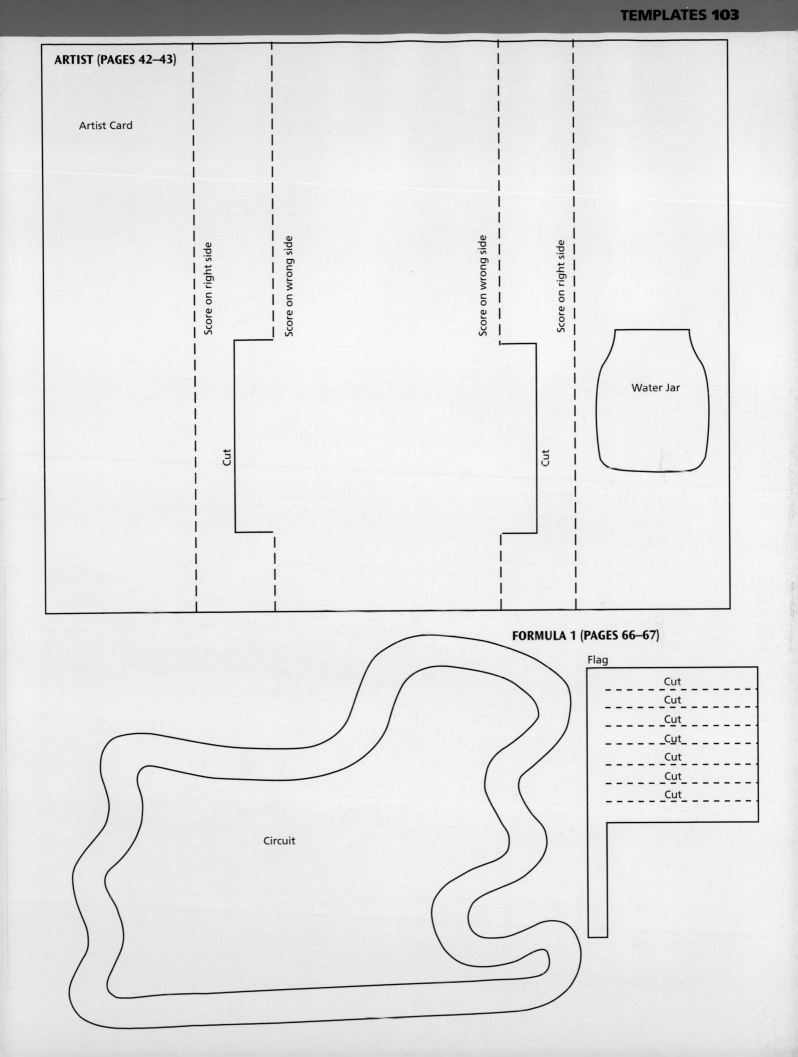

ARTIST (PAGES 42–43)

Artist Card

Score on right side

Score on wrong side

Score on wrong side

Score on right side

Cut

Cut

Water Jar

FORMULA 1 (PAGES 66–67)

Flag

Cut
Cut
Cut
Cut
Cut
Cut
Cut

Circuit

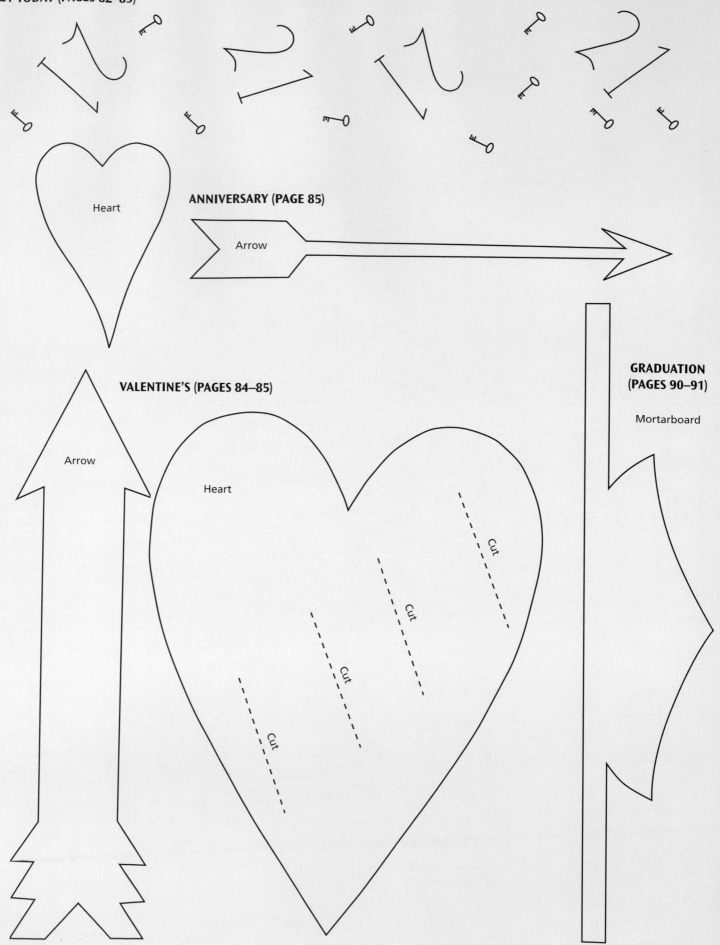

21 TODAY (PAGES 82–83)

Heart

ANNIVERSARY (PAGE 85)

Arrow

GRADUATION (PAGES 90–91)

Mortarboard

VALENTINE'S (PAGES 84–85)

Arrow

Heart

Cut

Cut

Cut

Cut

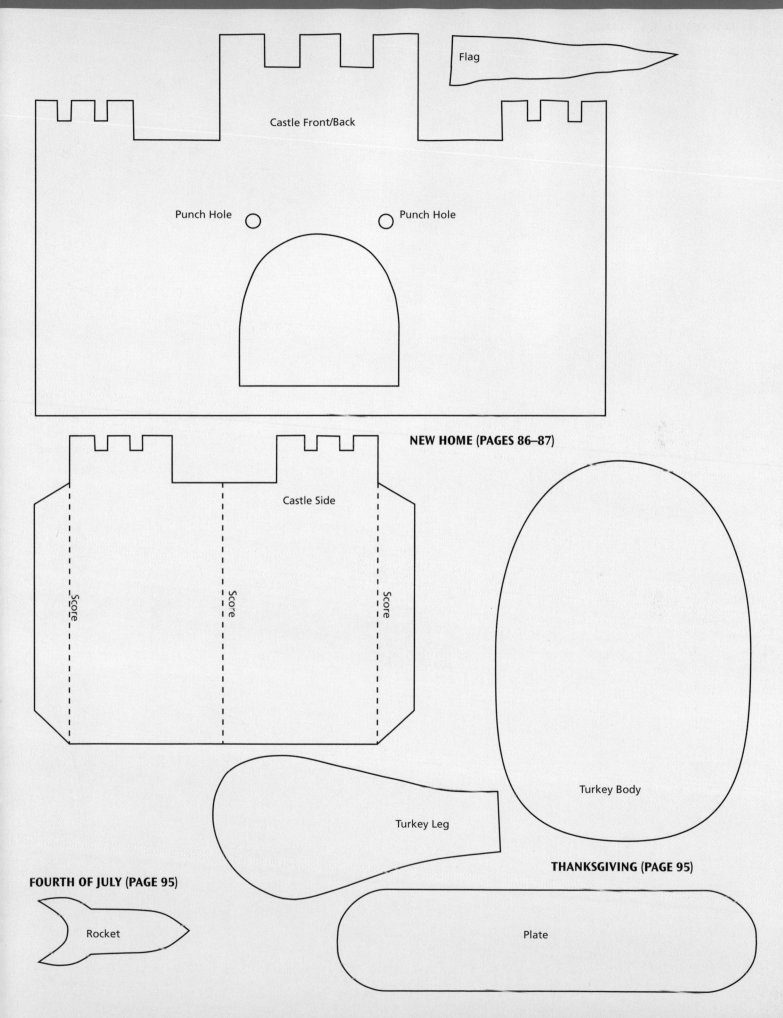

Flag

Castle Front/Back

Punch Hole   Punch Hole

NEW HOME (PAGES 86–87)

Castle Side

Score

Score

Score

Turkey Body

Turkey Leg

THANKSGIVING (PAGE 95)

FOURTH OF JULY (PAGE 95)

Rocket

Plate

NEW JOB (PAGE 87)

Briefcase

Front Pocket

Side Panels x 2

Fold

Fold

Fold

Handles x 2

Hole for Brad

Hole for Brad

Front and Back x 2

Front Flap

HORSERACING (PAGE 41)

Jockey Cap

Jockey Shirt

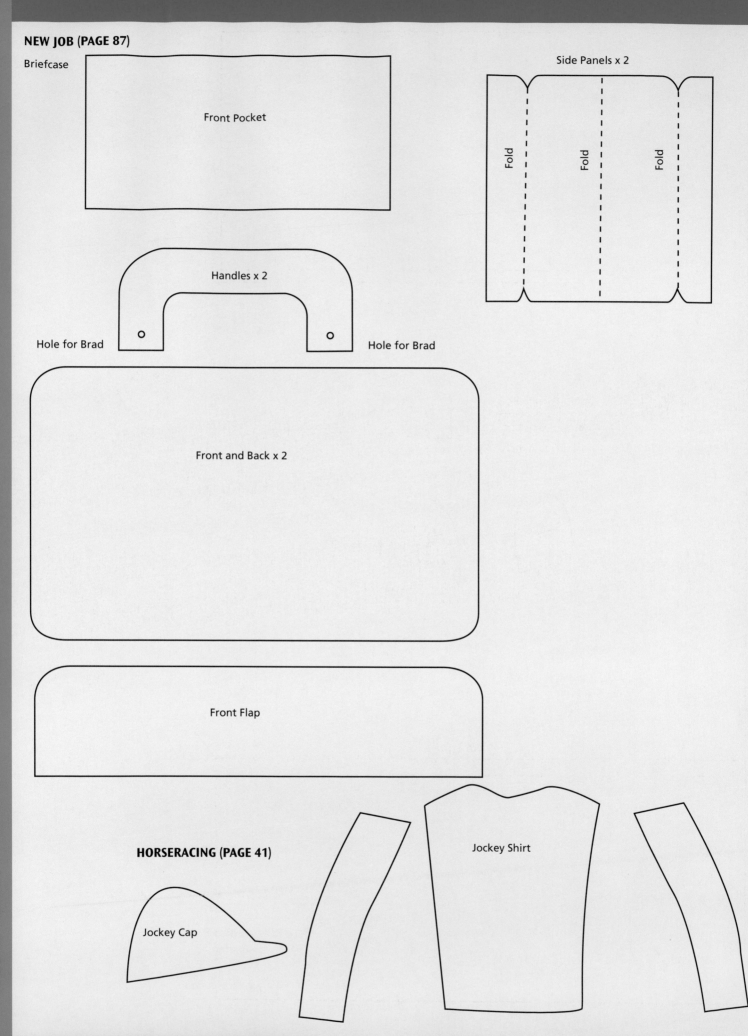

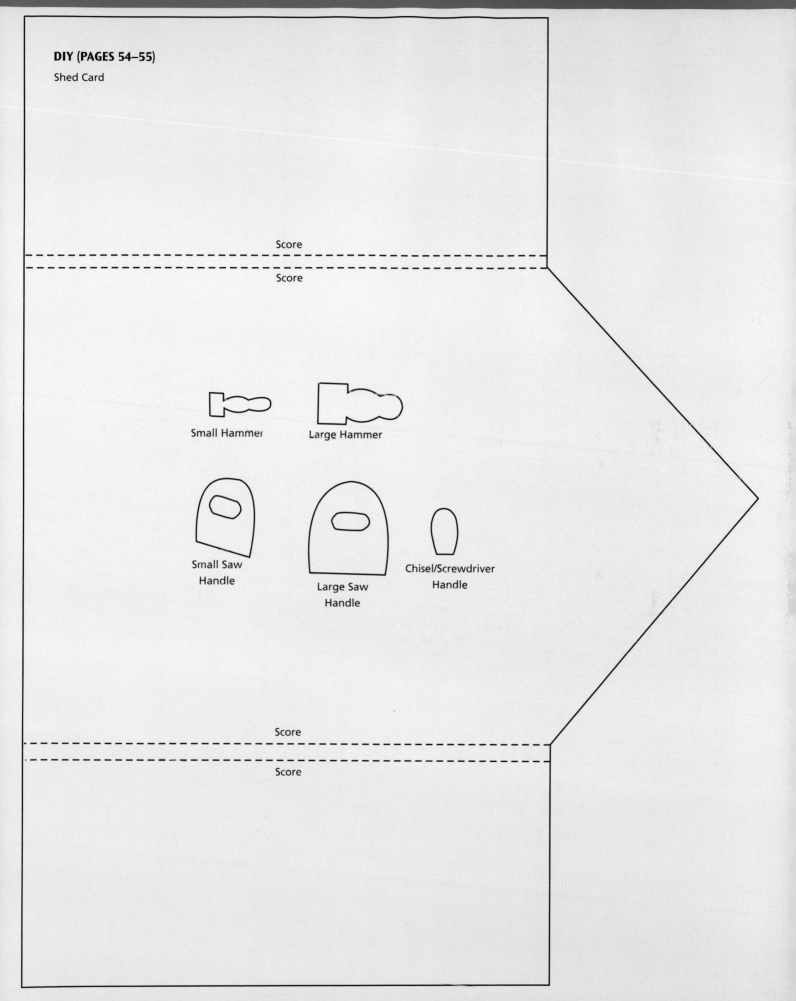

DIY (PAGES 54–55)

Shed Card

Score

Score

Small Hammer   Large Hammer

Small Saw
Handle

Large Saw
Handle

Chisel/Screwdriver
Handle

Score

Score

TEMPLATES ON THESE PAGES SHOWN AT 50% – ENLARGE ON A PHOTOCOPIER AT 200%

BOXING (PAGES 40)

Star Card

CARD BOX (PAGE 21)

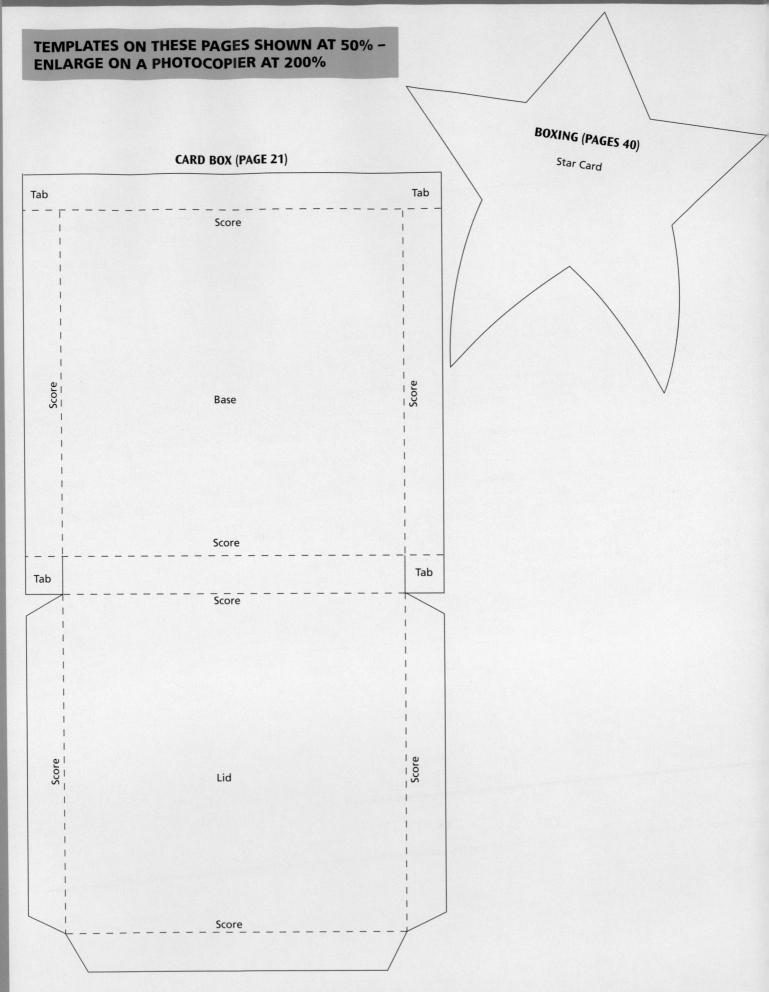

Tab

Tab

Score

Score

Score

Base

Score

Tab

Tab

Score

Score

Score

Lid

Score

Score

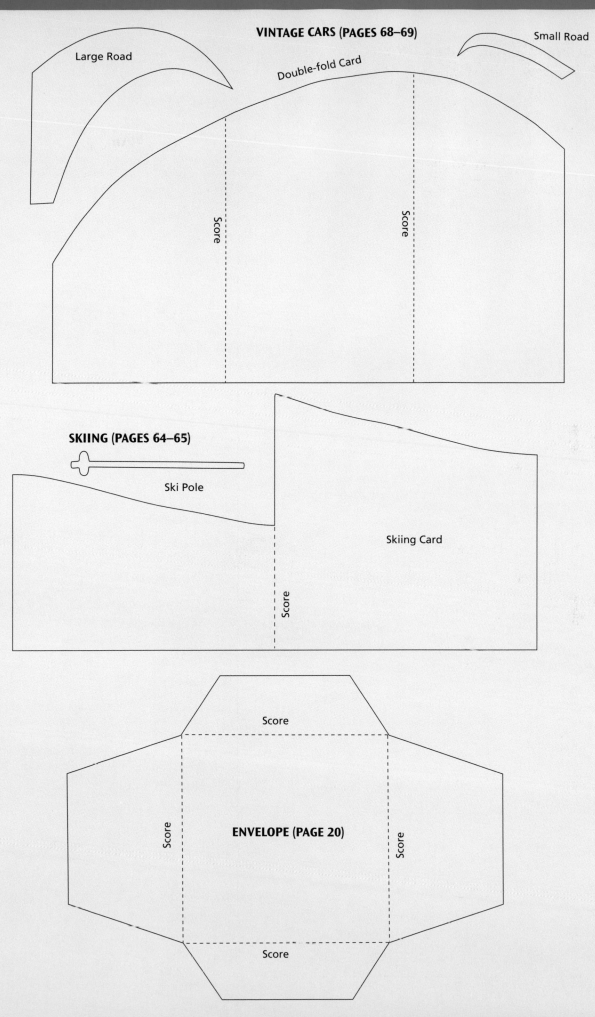

VINTAGE CARS (PAGES 68–69)

Large Road

Small Road

Double-fold Card

Score

Score

SKIING (PAGES 64–65)

Ski Pole

Skiing Card

Score

Score

Score

ENVELOPE (PAGE 20)

Score

Score

Score

MATERIALS

SOCCER (PAGES 24–25)
Soccer ball and soccer player peel-off stickers: XL425U black, XL679U blue, Craft Creations

CRICKET (PAGES 26–27)
Cricket découpage papers: DC157, Craft Creations
Cricket bat outline stamp: LT1310c, Hobby Art
Light brown inkpad: VersaMark™ Bisque

BASEBALL (PAGE 27)
Baseball peel-off stickers: 'Baseball Kids', Mambi Minis™; 'Baseball Sticker Borders', Sandylion Sticker Designs™

GOLF (PAGES 28–29)
Golf bag and clubs peel-off sticker: XL433U silver, Craft Creations

FISHING (PAGES 30–31)
Fishing embossed peel-off stickers: 'Fishing Images', K & Co

CYCLING (PAGE 33)
Black and white checked peel-off sticker: Creative Imaginations
Bicycle peel-off sticker: 'Extreme Riders' scrapbooking sticker sheet, www.starform.nl

MARTIAL ARTS (PAGES 36–37)
Oriental character printed paper: 'Characters Vellum', Heidi Grace Designs Inc
Karate peel-off stickers: 'Karate', Mrs Grossman's®

GOOD LUCK (PAGE 37)
Stencil: 'Lucky', American Traditional™
Oriental character printed paper: 'Characters Cardstock', Heidi Grace Designs Inc

ARTIST (PAGES 42–43)
Artists' materials peel-off stickers: XL137U black, Craft Creations

WINE (PAGES 44–45)
Vine corner stamp: 'Vine Corner' IN3075i, INCA Stamps (Personal Impressions™)
Green inkpad: VersaColour™ Tea Green
Crimson inkpad: Anna Griffin™
Stamp aligner: Woodware

MUSIC (PAGES 46–47)
Musical note peel-off stickers: XL136U gold-edged black, Craft Creations
Musical note rubber stamp: 'Musical Cleft', Whispers™
Solvent inkpad: StazOn® Jet Black

ROCK STAR (PAGE 47)
Drum kit peel-off stickers: 'Sports & Leisure Peel-Offs' Code 1632, Lakeland Limited

PHOTOGRAPHY (PAGE 49)
Camera peel-off sticker: 'Sports & Leisure Peel-Offs' Code 1632, Lakeland Limited
Patterned slide frame dome stickers: K & Co

COOKING (PAGES 50–51)
Square magnets: Impex Creative Crafts Ltd
Mini wooden rolling pin: Lara's Crafts

SNOOKER (PAGE 53)
Snooker peel-off stickers: XL432U black, Craft Creations

MANGA (PAGES 56–57)
Dual-tipped permanent marker pens: Letraset® ProMarker pens – Blush, Light Brown, Dark Brown, Green, Grey, Yellow, Blue, Pastel Blue
Bleedproof marker paper: Letraset® bleedproof maker paper
Silver number peel-off stickers: Anita's, DoCrafts
Musical note peel-off stickers: XL136U black, Craft Creations

PAINTBALLING (PAGES 60–61)
Camouflage printed paper: 'Camouflage, Wildlife Collection', Making Memories®
Black number peel-off stickers: Anita's, DoCrafts

GARDENING (PAGES 62–63)
Gardening collage printed paper: CS003, Craft Creations
Orange and green square brads: Making Memories®

SKIING (PAGES 64–65)
Tree shape fold and punch tool: Habico Ltd
Ski peel-off stickers: 'Hit the Slopes', Karen Foster Design Inc

SNOWBOARDING (PAGE 65)
Snowboard peel-off sticker: 'Hit the Slopes', Karen Foster Design Inc

FORMULA 1 (PAGES 66–67)
Silver and gold peel-off racing car stickers: Habico Ltd

VINTAGE CARS (PAGES 68–69)
Trees rubber stamp: Winter Trees 48654, Whispers™
Vintage car printed paper: 'sheet containing 10 different images of automotives and flying machines' 2062, Mamelok Press

SPORTS CARS (PAGE 69)
Sports car peel-off sticker: 'Sports & Leisure Peel-Offs' Code 1632, Lakeland Limited

HIKING (PAGE 71)
Footprint peel-off stickers: 'Hit the Trail', Karen Foster Design Inc

HOLIDAYS (PAGES 72–73)
Holiday peel-off stickers: XL068U black, Craft Creations
Palm tree rubber stamp: 'Palm Trees', The Stamp Bug Ltd
Metal camera charm: 'Metal Holiday Charms', Habico Ltd

STEAM TRAINS (PAGES 74–75)
Train printed paper: 'sheet containing 7 different images of trains' 2061, Mamelok Press
White puff paint: Dylon
Green plastic model foliage: Woodland Scenics

AEROPLANES (PAGE 75)
Aeroplanes printed paper: 'sheet containing 10 different images of automotives and flying machines' 2062, Mamelok Press

FATHER'S DAY (PAGES 78–79)
Pewter-finish hinges: Making Memories®

NEW DAD (PAGE 79)
Metal plaques: 'Charmed Plaques', 'Mini Baby', Making Memories®

70TH BIRTHDAY (PAGE 81)
Number peel-off stickers: XL407U green, Craft Creations

21 TODAY (PAGES 82–83)
Metal key embellishment: 'Life's Journey' metal keys, K & Co

VALENTINE'S (PAGES 84–85)
Lips rubber stamp: Lips 48018, Whispers™

CHRISTMAS (PAGES 88–89)
Lace® tree shape metal template: L2048

RETIREMENT (PAGES 92–93)
Printed papers: 'Artsy Collage', Masculine Paper Art Images 4311, Hot Off The Press™
Clock rubber stamp: 'Large Pocket Watch', Hampton Art Stamps

SUPPLIERS

The following information is correct at the time of going to press, but details are unavoidably subject to change.

UK

Centagraph
18 Station Parade,
Harrogate,
North Yorkshire HG1 1UE
tel: 01423 566327
www.centagraph.co.uk

Craft Creations Ltd
Ingersoll House,
Delamare Road, Cheshunt,
Hertfordshire EN8 9HD
tel: 01992 781900
www.craftcreations.co.uk

Craftwork Cards Ltd
Unit 7, The Moorings,
Waterside Road,
Stourton, Leeds,
West Yorkshire LS10 1DG
tel: 0113 276 5713
www.craftworkcards.com

DoCrafts
Design Objectives Ltd,
Unit 90, Woolsbridge
Industrial Park,
Three Legged Cross,
Wimborne,
Dorset BH21 6SU
tel: 01202 811000
www.docrafts.co.uk

Dylon International Ltd
Worsley Bridge Road,
Lower Sydenham,
London SE26 5HD
tel: 0208 663 4801
www.dylon.co.uk

Efco
Sinotex UK Ltd, Unit D,
The Courtyard Business
Centre, Lonesome Lane,
Reigate,
Surrey RH2 7QT
tel: 01737 245450
www.artys.co.uk

Fiskars UK Ltd
Newlands Avenue, Brackla
Industrial Estate, Bridgend,
Mid Glamorgan CF31 2XA
tel: 01656 655595
www.fiskars.com

**Glue Dots™
International Ltd**
Unit 1 Coronation Business
Park, Hard Ings Road,
Keighley, West Yorkshire
BD21 3ND
tel: 01535 616290
www.gluedotsuk.co.uk

Habico Ltd
Tong Road Industrial Estate,
Amberley Road,
Leeds LS12 4BD
tel: 0113 263 1500
www.habico.co.uk

Hobby Art
23 Holmethorpe Avenue,
Holmethorpe Industrial
Estate, Redhill,
Surrey RH1 2NL
tel: 01737 789977
email:
hobbyartstamps@fsmail.net

HobbyCraft Stores
tel: 0800 027 2387 for
nearest store or mail order
is available
www.hobbycraft.co.uk

Impex Creative Crafts Ltd
Impex House, Atlas Road,
Wembley, Middlesex
HA9 0TX
tel: 020 8900 0999
www.impexcreativecrafts.
co.uk

INCA Stamps (part of
Personal Impressions™)
See Personal Impressions™

**Jane Jenkins
Quilling Design**
33 Mill Rise, Skidby,
Cottingham,
East Yorkshire HU16 5UA
tel: 01482 843721
www.jjquilling.co.uk

Lakeland Limited
Alexandra Buildings,
Windermere,
Cumbria LA23 1BQ
tel: 015394 88100
www.lakelandlimited.com

Letraset Limited
Kingsnorth Industrial Estate,
Wotton Road, Ashford,
Kent TN23 6FL
tel: 01233 624421
www.letraset.com

Mamelok Press
Northern Way,
Bury St Edmunds,
Suffolk IP32 6NJ
tel: 01284 762291
www.mamelok.co.uk

Personal Impressions™
EM Richford Ltd,
Curzon Road,
Chilton Industrial Estate,
Sudbury CO10 2XW
tel: 01787 375241
www.richstamp.co.uk

PIJPOJ Limited
Unit G1, Apedale Road,
Apedale Business Park,
Newcastle Under Lyme,
Staffordshire ST5 6BH
tel: 01782 569620
www.pijpoj.co.uk

The Stamp Bug Ltd
Unit 3, The Old Sawmill
Workshops, Hatherop,
Near Cirencester,
Gloucester GL7 3NA
tel: 01285 750 308
www.thestampbug.co.uk

**Woodware Craft
Collection Ltd**
Unit 2a, Sandylands
Business Park, Skipton,
North Yorkshire BD23 2DE
tel: 01756 700024
email: sales@woodware.
co.uk

Xyron UK Ltd
Waterside House,
Cowley Business Park,
High Street, Cowley,
Uxbridge UB8 2HP
tel: 01895 878700
www.xyron.com

EUROPE

Kars Creative Wholesale
Industrieweg 27,
Industrieterrein 'De Heuning',
Postbus 97, 4050 EB
Ochten, The Netherlands
tel: +31 (0)344 642864
www.kars.nl

Starform
e-mail: info@starform.nl
fax: +31 (0)23 5570778
www.starform.nl

USA & CANADA

**American Traditional
Designs**
442 First NH Turnpike,
Northwood NH 03261
tel: 800 448 6656
www.americantraditional.
com

Anna Griffin Inc
2270 Marietta Boulevard,
Atlanta,
Georgia 30324
tel: 404 817 8170
www.annagriffin.com

Creative Imaginations
17832 Gothard Street,
Huntington Beach,
CA 92647
www.cigift.com

Dover Publications
Customer Care Department,
31 East 2nd Street,
Mineola, NY 11501–3852
www.doverpublications.com

Hampton Art Stamps
Hampton Art, LLC,
19 Industrial Boulevard,
Medford, New York 11763
tel: 800 229 1019
www.hamptonart.com

Heidi Grace Designs
(part of Fiskars)
tel: 866 348 5661
www.fiskars.com

Hot Off The Press Inc
1250 NW Third,
Canby OR 97013
tel: 888 300 3406
www.paperwishes.com

JudiKins Inc
17803 S Harvard Boulevard,
Gardena, CA 90248
tel: 310 515 1115
www.judikins.com

K & Co
8500 N W River Park Drive,
Pillar #136, Parkville,
MO 64152
tel: 888 244 2083
www.kandcompany.com

Karen Foster Design Inc
623 North 1250 West,
Centerville, Utah 84014
tel: 801 451 9779
www.karenfosterdesign.com

Lara's Crafts
4220 Clay Avenue,
Fort Worth, TX 76117
Toll-Free Sales: 800 232 5272
tel: 817 581 5210
www.larascrafts.com

Making Memories®
1168 West 500 North,
Centerville, Utah 84014
tel: 801 294 0430
www.makingmemories.com

**MAMBI
(me & my BIG ideas®)**
20321 Valencia Circle,
Lake Forest, CA 92630
tel: 949 583 2065
(wholesale only)
www.meandmybigideas.com

Michaels' Stores
8000 Bent Branch Drive,
Irving, TX 75063
tel: 800 642 4235
www.michaels.com

Mrs Grossman's
MGPC, P O Box 4467,
Petaluma, CA 94955
tel: 800 429 4549
www.mrsgrossmans.com

**Sandylion
Sticker Designs™**
400 Cochrane Drive,
Markham, Ontario L3R8E3
tel: 905 475 0523
www.sandylion.com

Sugarloaf Products Inc
See www.
sugarloafproducts.com
for retailers of Whispers™
and Anita's Art Stamps and
Anita's Art peel-off stickers

Tsukineko, Inc
17640 NE 65th Street,
Redmond, WA 98052
tel: 425 883 7733
See www.tsukineko.com
for stockists of VersaMark™
and StazOn™

Woodland Scenics
PO Box 98, Linn Creek,
MO 65052
tel: 573 346 5555
www.woodlandscenics.com

INDEX

ABOUT THE AUTHOR

Elizabeth Moad has practised crafts for several years, attending craft fairs and regularly contributing to crafts magazines. Her passion for art and crafts led her to undertake further study in order to pursue a creative career, and she has recently completed a BA Degree in Fine Arts. She is author of *The Papercrafter's Bible*, also published by David & Charles. Elizabeth lives in Ipswich, East Anglia, in the UK.

ACKNOWLEDGMENTS

Many thanks to Cheryl Brown, Jennifer Proverbs, Ali Myer and Sarah Clark of David & Charles. Special thanks to Jo Richardson, Karl Adamson and my family and friends for their support.